The Modern
Jewish Experience

The Modern
Jewish Experience

Advisory Editor

Moses Rischin

Editorial Board

Arthur A. Goren

Irving Howe

ECONOMIC CONDITION OF THE JEWS IN RUSSIA

Isaac M. Rubinow

ARNO PRESS

A New York Times Company

New York / 1975

Reprint Edition 1975 by Arno Press Inc.

Reprinted from a copy in
  The University of Illinois Library

THE MODERN JEWISH EXPERIENCE
ISBN for complete set: 0-405-06690-2
See last pages of this volume for titles.

Manufactured in the United States of America

————•◦•————

Library of Congress Cataloging in Publication Data

Rubinow, Issac Max, 1875-1936.
    Economic condition of the Jews in Russia.

    (The Modern Jewish experience)
    Reprint of the 1907 ed. published by the U. S. Govt.
Print Off., Washington, and issued as Bulletin v. 15 of
U. S. Bureau of Labor.
    1. Jews in Russia--Economic conditions. 2. Russia--
Economic conditions. I. Title. II. Series.
III. Series: United States. Bureau of Labor Statistics.
Bulletin ; v. 15.
DS135.R9R73 1975   331.6'3'924047   74-29519
ISBN 0-405-06744-5

ECONOMIC CONDITION OF THE JEWS IN RUSSIA.

BY I. M. RUBINOW.

INTRODUCTION.

The present study of the economic condition of the Jews in Russia is offered as a part of a series of studies on immigration and its relation to social and industrial questions in the United States. One of the most important elements in this problem is the distribution, both geographically and industrially, of immigrants arriving in this country. A study of immigration at the present time would not be complete without special attention to the Russian Jews, forming as they do one-eighth of the total number of immigrants now coming to our shores, and being found so frequently living and working under harmful sweat-shop conditions. Some of the well-known characteristics of these immigrants, such as their tendency to crowd into the great cities and to follow certain definite lines of work to the exclusion of the heavier manual trades and agriculture, will be much better understood after a study of the conditions and restrictions under which they have worked and lived before coming to this country.

JEWISH POPULATION.

As far back as authentic historic records go, Jews are known to have lived within the territory at present included in the limits of the Russian Empire, yet the Russian Empire as it now exists acquired the vast majority of its Jewish citizens at a comparatively recent date. Until 1772 the number of Jews in Russia proper was small, because until then the absolutely prohibitive policy of the Russian Government made any movement across the Polish-Russian frontier practically impossible. The gradual migration of the Jews eastward through Europe resulted in concentrating a large number in the Kingdom of Poland, in which country and in Lithuania Jews are known to have lived as early as the tenth century. The first partition of Poland, in 1792, gave to Russia the section known as White Russia and a part of Lithuania, with a large Jewish population; the second partition, in 1793, and the final partition, in 1795, added the ten Provinces which now constitute the so-called region of the Vistula. Since those events the Russian Empire has remained the home of at least one-half of the

487

entire Jewish race.   While the total number of Jews in the world is not definitely known, the estimate of 11,000,000 is usually accepted as nearly correct.   According to the Russian census of January 28 (February 9), 1897, the total number of Jews in the Empire was 5,215,805 [a] or about 50 per cent of all the Jews in the world.   Since the total population of the Empire has been determined to be 125,640,021, the proportion of the Jewish to the total population is therefore only a little over 4 per cent; but this percentage has little more than a theoretical value, because of the very uneven distribution of the Jews over the entire territory of the Empire.   The policy of the Muscovite Government toward the Jews throughout the sixteenth, seventeenth, and eighteenth centuries was that of absolute exclusion, and with a few qualifications the same policy has been enforced within the annexed western territories, which contain the large Jewish population.   The law of 1769 definitely limited the Jew's right of domicile to certain Provinces, thus establishing the strictly defined Jewish Pale, that law being modified in 1804 by the inclusion of several Provinces and the exclusion of others.   Several modifications of minor significance have been made in subsequent years.   The Pale as it exists to-day was established in 1835 by the "Code of the rights of the Jews."   As thus constituted, the Pale consists of twenty-five Provinces [b] of the eighty-nine Provinces and Territories consti-

---

a The problem of determining the number of Jews in Russia presents some serious statistical difficulties, depending upon the different definitions of the word "Jew."   In the census of 1897 both the religion and the nationality were taken account of, the latter being based upon the "mother tongue."   In the case of the Jews the "Yiddish language" was taken as the decisive feature.   Accordingly, the following conflicting statements may be formed: Number of persons of Jewish religion, 5,215,805; number of persons of Jewish nationality as determined by the mother tongue, 5,063,156.   A closer examination of the census figures shows that there were enumerated 161,505 persons of Jewish faith who named other languages than the Yiddish as their mother tongue.   On the other hand, there were 8,856 persons speaking the Yiddish tongue whose religious faith was other than the Hebrew.   As the special legislation in regard to Jews applies to all persons of Jewish faith, 5,215,805 ought to be accepted as the correct figure.   Yet in the census many important tables take the nationality (language) basis.   The 12,894 Karaites (people of Jewish nationality and faith, but of a different sect and exempt from all special Jewish legislation) must not be disregarded; of these 383 claimed Yiddish as their mother tongue and are therefore included in the preceding groups. The data therefore may be summarized thus:

Persons of Jewish faith claiming Yiddish as their mother tongue........... 5, 054, 300
Persons of Jewish faith claiming other languages as their mother tongue.... 161, 505
Persons of other faiths claiming Yiddish as their mother tongue........... 8, 856
Karaites claiming other languages than Yiddish 12, 511

Total.. 5, 237, 172

It is necessary to add that often in special tables of the census the total number of Jews indicated does not agree with either of the totals given here.

b The Russian word "gubernia" has often been translated into English as "government," under the influence of the French translation "gouvernement."   In view of the misleading nature of this term the word "province" is here preferred.

tuting the entire Russian Empire. The Pale begins immediately south of the Baltic Provinces, stretches throughout the west, and extends over the south as far east as the Don Army Territory. The combined territory of the Pale is about 362,000 square miles, or less than 20 per cent of European Russia and only a little over 4 per cent of the entire Russian Empire. The Pale includes:

1. In the Kingdom of Poland (or the region of the Vistula), the Provinces of Warsaw, Kalisz, Kielce, Lomza, Lublin, Petrikau, Plock, Radom, Suvalki, and Siedlec.

2. In Lithuania, the Provinces of Vilna, Kovno, and Grodno.

3. In White Russia, the Provinces of Minsk, Vitebsk, and Moheelev.

4. In southwestern Russia, the Provinces of Volhynia, Podolia, Kiev (except the city of Kiev), Chernigov, and Poltava.

5. In southern (new) Russia, the Provinces of Bessarabia, Kherson, Yekaterinoslav, and Taurida (except the city of Yalta).

At various times many modifications of the absolute prohibition to enter the interior of Russia were made; but the entire Russian legislation in regard to the Jew's right of domicile is much too complicated to be given in detail, and consequently only the main features will be stated. Its essential principle is that, while the general prohibition remains in force, the following specified classes of Jews are given the privilege of domicile throughout the Empire:

1. Merchants of the first guild—i. e., merchants paying a very high business license—after having paid that license somewhere within the Pale for five consecutive years. This right of living anywhere in Russia, outside of the Pale, lasts only as long as the payment of the license is continued, but after ten annual payments the permanent right of domicile within the city in which the payments have been made is acquired.

2. Professional persons, such as physicians, lawyers, dentists, graduate engineers, army surgeons, midwives, and graduates of universities and higher institutions of learning in general, as well as students in such institutions.

3. Master-artisans working at their trades when admitted to their artisans' guild, or possessing the necessary legal evidence of proficiency in their crafts.

In all these cases the acquired right of domicile extends to the members of the immediate family, and in cases of the merchants of the first guild and the professional persons to a limited number of servants and clerks of Jewish faith. In regard to the Jewish artisans, the limitations are much more numerous; and in 1891 their further emigration from the Pale into the interior of the Empire was made exceedingly difficult, and those artisans who were living in the city, as well as those living in the Province of Moscow, were compelled to withdraw.

Another considerable class of Jews that is permitted to live throughout Russia are the discharged soldiers; but this right is granted only to those who served in the army prior to 1874. This class, therefore, can not increase in number.

Besides these general provisions, there are minor exceptions that grant to limited groups of Jews (usually determined as persons or descendants of persons who were living in certain localities before certain dates) the right to remain in specified localities, or, in a few cases, anywhere in the Empire. Among these exceptions are to be found the resident Jews of Siberia, Turkestan, Caucasus, the Province of Courland, and a few other localities.

The temporary sojourn without the Pale of Jews who have no right of permanent domicile is strictly limited by law to from six weeks to two months, and then only in cases of proved necessity, such as a lawsuit, commercial transactions, or probating a will. Moreover, in these cases important limitations have been introduced. Thus, the important city of Kiev has been excepted from the Pale, and even merchants of the first guild may live only in certain districts of that city. In 1893 the city of Yalta was excepted, and the important cities of Rostov and Taganrog, by being transferred from the Province of Yekaterinoslav to the Don Army Territory, were also excluded from the Pale.[a]

How well the object of this legislation was accomplished will be seen from the following official data:

TOTAL POPULATION OF RUSSIA AND NUMBER AND PER CENT OF JEWS, WITH PER CENT OF DISTRIBUTION OF JEWS, BY LOCALITIES, 1897.

[Compiled from Premier Recensement Général de la Population de l'Empire de Russie, 1897.]

Locality.	Total population.	Persons of Jewish faith.	Per cent of Jews of total population.	Per cent of distribution of Jews.
Fifteen Provinces of Pale	32,936,314	3,578,327	10.9	68.6
The remaining 35 Provinces	60,506,550	211,121	.3	4.0
Total European Russia, proper	93,442,864	3,789,448	4.1	72.6
Kingdom of Poland	9,402,253	1,321,100	14.1	25.3
Caucasus	9,289,364	56,783	.6	1.1
Siberia	5,758,822	34,792	.6	.7
Middle Asia	7,746,718	13,682	.2	.3
Total	125,640,021	5,215,805	4.2	100.0

Of all the Jews residing in the vast Russian Empire, 93.9 per cent live in the Pale (including the 10 Polish Provinces), 4.0 per cent live in the remaining part of European Russia, and 2.1 per cent live in all

---

[a] See M. J. Mysh, Rukowodstvo k Russkym zakonam o evreakh (Handbook of Russian legislation in regard to Jews). St. Petersburg, 1904.

the Asiatic possessions of the Empire. The Jews, therefore, constitute almost a negligible part of the population of Russia beyond the Pale. Hence the present study will naturally be devoted almost exclusively to the economic conditions within the Pale. Even within that limited area, the Jews constitute only 11.6 per cent, or about one-ninth, of the entire population. The proportion varies considerably from one Province or region to another, and the reasons for this variation are not difficult to find when the historical line of migration of the Jews is taken into consideration. The southern Provinces, having been thrown open to the Jews at a comparatively recent date, have a smaller percentage of people of that race than has either Poland or Lithuania.

TOTAL POPULATION AND NUMBER AND PER CENT OF JEWISH POPULATION OF THE PALE, BY PROVINCES, 1897.

[Compiled from Premier Recensement Général de la Population de l'Empire de Russie, 1897.]

Province or region.	Total population.	Persons of Jewish faith.	
		Number.	Per cent of total population.
Vilna	1,591,207	204,686	12.9
Grodno	1,603,409	280,489	17.5
Kovno	1,544,564	212,666	13.8
Lithuania	4,739,180	697,841	14.7
Minsk	2,147,621	345,015	16.1
Vitebsk	1,489,246	175,629	11.8
Moheelev	1,686,764	203,946	12.1
White Russia	5,323,631	724,590	13.6
Volhynia	2,989,482	395,882	13.2
Podolia	3,018,299	370,612	12.3
Kiev	3,559,229	433,728	12.2
Chernigov	2,297,854	114,452	5.0
Poltava	2,778,151	110,944	4.0
Southwestern Russia	14,643,015	1,425,618	9.7
Bessarabia	1,935,412	228,528	11.8
Kherson	2,733,612	339,910	12.4
Yekaterinoslav	2,113,674	101,088	4.8
Taurida	1,447,790	60,752	4.2
Southern (new) Russia	8,230,488	730,278	9.0
Warsaw	1,931,867	351,942	18.2
Kalisz	840,597	71,657	8.5
Kielce	761,995	83,221	10.9
Lomza	579,592	91,394	15.8
Lublin	1,160,662	156,221	13.5
Petrikau	1,403,901	222,558	15.9
Plock	553,633	51,454	9.3
Radom	814,947	112,323	13.8
Suvalki	582,913	59,195	10.2
Siedlec	772,146	121,135	15.7
Poland	9,402,253	1,321,100	14.1
Total in Pale	42,338,567	4,899,427	11.6

The Jews living in Lithuania, as well as those who live in White Russia, are known as Lithuanian Jews; the Jews of the ten Polish

Provinces as Polish Jews, and those who have settled in the southwestern region and in New Russia as southern Jews. From the American point of view ihe distinctions are not without some practical significance, because the Lithuanian Jews have until recently constituted the vast majority of the Russian-Jewish immigrants to the United States. The general culture of the Polish Jews is considerably lower than that of the Lithuanian Jews. The economic condition of the Jews in the south of Russia is so much better than that of those in the northwest that only since the recent disturbances has the emigration fever touched the Jews of that region. Of all the Jews in the Empire, the northwestern Jews, comprising those in Lithuania and White Russia, constitute 27.3 per cent, the Polish Jews 25.3 per cent, or approximately the same proportion, and the southern Jews, comprising those in southwestern and southern (new) Russia, 41.3 per cent.

Travelers through western Russia have seldom failed to point out the awful congestion of Jews in the cities and towns. The census of 1897 shows, however, that the Jews constitute only from 8 to 18 per cent of the total population of the several provinces. This concentration of the Jews in cities and towns is due to the so-called "May Laws," promulgated on May 3 (15), 1882, as a result of the series of anti-Jewish riots in 1881, which prohibited further settlement of Jews within rural districts, i. e., outside of cities and towns. In practice this meant not only prohibition of further emigration of Jews from cities into the country, but an actual elimination of many Jewish households from rural settlements, and their enforced migration into towns and the resultant congestion of the latter. The tendency of the modern age everywhere is toward emigration from the rural districts to the city; the Jewish race, however, has lived under very exceptional conditions and for centuries has inhabited the cities almost exclusively. With the general decline of the prosperity of the Russian and Polish nobility, the making of a living became more difficult for the Jew and this led to a moderate though unmistakable tendency to remove to the rural districts. Thither went the petty merchant, the liquor dealer, the artisan, and finally the prospective Jewish agriculturalist. The May laws not only stopped this movement but forced many of the Jewish families already in the country back into cities. Again, in 1891, thousands of families of Jewish artisans and merchants were forced to leave the city of Moscow and other interior cities and seek new homes in the cities of the Pale. Both the May laws of 1882 and the new executive orders of 1891 caused a considerable increase in the emigration of Jews to the United States.

The proportion of the Jewish population to the total population of the cities of the Pale is shown in the following table:

JEWISH URBAN POPULATION COMPARED WITH TOTAL URBAN POPULATION IN THE PALE, BY REGIONS, 1897.

[Compiled from Premier Recensement Général de la Population de l'Empire de Russie, 1897.]

Region.	Total urban population.	Jewish urban population.	
		Number.	Per cent of total urban population.
Lithuania	595,742	297,980	50.0
White Russia	588,051	324,847	55.2
Southwestern Russia	1,398,717	502,830	35.9
Southern (new) Russia	1,612,613	453,980	28.2
Poland	2,158,662	813,375	37.7
Total	6,353,785	2,393,012	37.7

These data must be taken with many qualifications, for a great deal of uncertainty exists in regard to the Russian definition of the city. Many localities not dignified by the name of "gorod" (city) are known as "miestechko," and in these settlements the Jews have retained the right of domicile. These "miestechkos" have the economic function of the American village—i. e., they serve as the commercial, and, to a small degree, the industrial centers of the surrounding country. The Russian village, as is well known, is usually an agricultural community, and in these villages the Jew is prohibited from settling.

Interesting data that throw some light upon the concentration of Jews within the cities and the "miestechkos" have been gathered by the agents of the St. Petersburg committee of the Jewish Colonization Society.([a]) According to the reports of these agents, the urban Jewish population of the Pale at the end of the nineteenth century amounted to 3,809,361, or 77.8 per cent of the total Jewish population of the Pale in 1897.

JEWISH URBAN POPULATION IN THE PALE IN 1898 COMPARED WITH TOTAL JEWISH POPULATION IN THE PALE IN 1897, BY REGIONS.

[The figures for 1897 are from Premier Recensement Général de la Population de l'Empire de Russie; those for 1898 are from the Report of the Jewish Colonization Society.]

Region.	Total Jewish population (1897).	Jewish urban population (1898).	
		Number.	Per cent of total Jewish population (1897).
Northwestern Russia (Lithuania and White Russia)	1,422,431	1,213,054	85.3
Southwestern Russia	1,425,618	978,406	68.6
Southern (new) Russia	730,278	511,487	70.0
Poland	1,321,100	1,106,414	83.7
Total	4,899,427	3,809,361	77.8

[a] In 1898 an extensive investigation into the economic condition of the Russian Jews was undertaken by agents of the society. As a result of these investigations two volumes were published in the spring of 1905, entitled "Sbornik Materialov ob Economicheskom Polozhenii Evreev v Rossii" (Collection of material in regard to the economic condition of the Jews in Russia). These volumes contain a wealth of statistical information which has been freely used in this study. In fact the statistical data have been taken from these volumes unless otherwise credited.

In the following table is given the percentage which the urban Jews form of the total numbers of Jews in each region embraced within the Pale as shown by the census of 1897. The figures relate only to those cities that are incorporated:

JEWISH POPULATION OF INCORPORATED CITIES COMPARED WITH TOTAL JEWISH POPULATION IN THE PALE, BY REGIONS, 1897.

[Compiled from Premier Recensement Général de la Population de l'Empire de Russie, 1897.]

Region.	Total Jewish population.	Jewish population in incorporated cities.	
		Number.	Per cent of total Jewish population.
Lithuania	697,841	297,980	42.7
White Russia	724,590	324,847	44.8
Southwestern Russia	1,425,618	502,830	35.3
Southern (new) Russia	730,278	453,980	62.2
Poland	1,321,100	813,375	61.6
Total	4,899,427	2,393,012	48.8

It is almost certain that the data obtained in the private investigation are far from complete, and that the proportion of Jews living outside of the urban communities is considerably smaller than one-fifth. It is characteristic that the percentage of Jews living in rural districts is highest in the west and in the southwest, where, as will be shown, the Jews have attained considerable success in agricultural pursuits and where their general economic position is better. Of those Jews who have taken advantage of the right to migrate from their old homes in Poland and in Lithuania to the new region, a large proportion has evidently preferred the country to the city. This is significant as additional evidence of the fact (if additional evidence were necessary) that the remarkable concentration of Jews in the city is not a result of economic choice, or even economic necessity, but of enforced legislative limitations.

As was stated before, the Jews were a commercial and industrial race before they arrived in Poland, and therefore a strong element in urban population; but perhaps nowhere else have they become such a large part of the urban population as in western Russia.

JEWISH POPULATION COMPARED WITH TOTAL POPULATION OF CITIES INVESTIGATED BY JEWISH COLONIZATION SOCIETY, BY REGIONS, 1898.

Region.	Total population of cities investigated.	Jewish population of cities investigated.	
		Number.	Per cent of total population.
Northwestern Russia	2,093,259	1,213,054	57.9
Southwestern Russia	2,565,763	978,406	38.1
Southern (new) Russia	1,945,379	511,487	26.3
Poland	2,702,846	1,106,414	40.9
Total	9,307,247	3,809,361	40.9

The difference between these data and those of the official census is explained by the development of large cities both in Poland (Warsaw, Lodz, etc.) and in the south (Odessa and others). The Jewish "miestechko," with its economic stagnation and almost total absence of industry, is characteristic of the northwestern provinces. These little towns supply a large number of the Jewish emigrants to the United States.

The greatest congestion is found in the six northwestern provinces, where the Jews constitute almost three-fifths of the population of the cities. In Poland the recent development of textile industries has attracted to the cities a considerable element of German and Polish workingmen, while the mechanical, iron, and mining industries of the south have drawn upon the surrounding Russian peasantry. The congestion of Jews in the cities of Lithuania has been most acutely felt, especially since the May laws of 1882 and the stringent regulations of 1891, and it is, therefore, no coincidence that the region which shows the greatest percentage of Jews in cities also gives the greatest number of emigrants. Scarcely a Jewish family can be found in Lithuania that has not some members in the New World.

It must be remembered that the census data refer to the beginning of 1897, i. e., ten years ago. The well-known fecundity of the Jewish race on the one hand and the vast migratory element on the other must have introduced many important changes in the statistics of Jewish population, which can not be ascertained with any degree of accuracy. The census of 1897 was the first actual enumeration of population ever undertaken by the Russian Government, and it is therefore impossible to determine even the rate of increase. An official determination of the Jewish population was, however, made for Poland in 1890 and for the remaining fifteen provinces of the Pale in 1881, which gives some basis for comparison of the Jewish population at these dates with that of 1897, and upon which the approximate rate of increase may be computed.

JEWISH POPULATION IN THE PALE IN 1881 AND 1897, WITH NUMBER AND PER CENT OF INCREASE, BY REGIONS.

[The figures for 1881 and those for Poland in 1890 are taken from official publications of the Russian ministry of the interior.]

Region.	1881.	1897.	Increase in 16 years.	
			Number.	Per cent.
Northwestern Russia	1,243,007	1,422,431	179,424	14.4
Southwestern Russia	1,215,393	1,425,618	210,225	17.3
Southern Russia	453,765	730,278	276,513	60.9
Total	2,912,165	3,578,327	666,162	22.9
Poland	a 1,134,268	1,321,100	b 186,832	b 16.5

a In 1890.   b Increase in 7 years.

An increase of 22.9 per cent during sixteen years equals about 1.4 per cent per year, a very moderate increase indeed. In Poland the increase (during seven years) in absolute figures was greater than in northwestern Russia during a period more than twice as long, the average annual increase being about 2.4 per cent. The average annual increase in northwestern Russia was less than 1 per cent. This remarkable difference is undoubtedly due to emigration, not only to foreign lands, but also to the southern provinces, since the growth of the number of Jews in the south by 60.9 per cent in sixteen years would have been impossible without considerable immigration from the northwestern region. There is some migration from Lithuania into the industrial region of Poland, notably the textile district of Lodz, but it is not very large, and there is probably a correspondingly large emigration of Polish Jews to the United States. The rate of increase shown by the Jews in Poland may, therefore, be considered fairly normal. The natural annual increase of the Jewish population in Russia would seem to amount to at least 100,000 or 110,000 persons, and in the ten years which have passed since the census of 1897 to a little over 1,000,000, but emigration must have considerably reduced this increase. The number of Russian-Jewish emigrants to the United States alone amounted to many hundreds of thousands, and there was a considerable emigration of Russian Jews to Great Britain, while slighter currents carried them to many other countries of the civilized world. At present the emigration to the United States alone is sufficient to offset the entire natural increase, the total emigration possibly causing a reduction of the Jewish population in Russia, not only in relative but in absolute figures. The last two years, however, were abnormal in a great many ways and can not be considered a fair measure of the normal Russian-Jewish emigration. During the years 1898 to 1902 the emigration was considerably smaller, and it may safely be assumed that the total Jewish population in Russia at present is about 5,500,000.

No less significant is the tendency of the Jewish population toward wider distribution. It has been shown above that the increase in southern (new) Russia was considerably greater than in the rest of the Pale. The comparison with the increase of the non-Jewish population emphasizes this point.

PER CENT OF INCREASE OF NON-JEWISH AND JEWISH POPULATION IN 15 PROVINCES OF THE PALE, 1881 TO 1897.

Region.	Per cent of increase.	
	Non-Jewish.	Jewish.
Northwestern Russia	22.7	14.4
Southwestern Russia	22.3	17.3
Southern (new) Russia	37.8	60.9
Total	26.0	22.9

Another investigator has subdivided the Provinces of the Pale (exclusive of Poland) into western, middle, and eastern Provinces, with the following results: ([a])

In five western Provinces the Jewish population increased 7.5 per cent; in four middle Provinces the Jewish population increased 29.3 per cent; in six eastern Provinces the Jewish population increased 46.8 per cent.

Notwithstanding the legal difficulties, the eastward pressure of the Jewish population is clearly felt within the limits rigidly prescribed by the Government. This in itself suffices to explain why of all the special legislation affecting the Jew that which limited his right of domicile caused bitter complaints even many years before the present acute struggle for the emancipation of the Jew began. If it be remembered that 125,000 Jews found the means to emigrate to the United States within one year—though the voyage requires considerable capital—it will be understood that upon the destruction of legal barriers there would follow a considerable migration to the interior of Russia, where the prizes offered to business enterprise or skilled trades are no smaller than in the United States. Still stronger is the tendency toward removal to the rural districts, as such movement means a closer proximity to the natural customer of the commercial and the industrial Jew. Notwithstanding the strict supervision exercised by the authorities, the efforts of the Jew to enter the forbidden regions in circumvention of existing legislation are frequent and persistent.

At first glance there appears to be no valid reason why the simple fact of the ethnic and religious homogeneity of 40, 50, or even 60 per cent of the population of some cities of western Russia should be considered a cause of economic distress. But when the involuntary nature of this concentration is understood the problem becomes much clearer.

OCCUPATIONS.

The historical origin of the strict Jewish exclusion laws is to be found in the spirit of religious antagonism which was perfectly natural in the stage of culture that existed in Russia before the nineteenth century. On the other hand, the spirit of isolation which was strong in the Jew of Poland and Lithuania was no less an obstacle to the diffusion of the Jewish population throughout Russia. During the first three-quarters of the nineteenth century gradual efforts were made on both sides to break down the wall between

[a] See Sbornik Materialov ob Economicheskom Polozhenii Evreev v Rossii (Collection of material in regard to the economic condition of the Jews in Russia). Vol. I, page xxxiv.

the Jews and the Russians. The Government recognized the advisability of utilizing the commercial talents, the industrial enterprise, and the professional skill of the Jew, which were to some degree lacking in the mass of the Russian people. Western culture gradually forced its way into the Jewish communities and for a time the ideal of Russification had most ardent supporters in the Jewish young generation. Since 1875 the conditions have considerably changed. The Jewish right of domicile throughout Russia has been subject to further limitations, as already mentioned, and these are defended on entirely different grounds. The religious argument was laid aside and the economic argument emphasized instead. The argument is that the entire Jewish race is a race of traders, and therefore exploiters, and that the free admission of the Jews into the interior of Russia would be to the extreme disadvantage of the entire Russian nation. It is argued that when inclosed within the narrow limits of the Pale and enjoined from entering the villages the injury of the exploiting Jew to the economic well-being of the Russian peasant would be reduced to a minimum. This line of argument has been circulated even beyond the boundaries of Russia and undoubtedly not without some influence upon the public mind. This makes the data in regard to the occupations of the Russian Jews important and doubly interesting.

TOTAL JEWISH POPULATION AND NUMBER ENGAGED IN GAINFUL OCCUPATIONS, BY OCCUPATIONS, 1897.

[From the Premier Recensement Général de la Population de l'Empire de Russie, 1897.]

Class No.	Occupation.	Persons engaged in gainful occupations.			Members of their families.	Total.
		Male.	Female.	Total.		
1	Administration, justice, and police	890	18	908	2,609	3,517
2	Municipal and local civil service............	1,667	12	1,679	5,844	7,523
3	Private law practice.....................	1,028	9	1,037	3,268	4,305
4	Army and navy	53,194	....	53,194	1,083	54,277
5	Clergymen, orthodox.....................	173	21	194	510	704
6	Clergymen, other Christian...............	82	2	84	204	288
7	Clergymen, non-Christian.................	6,030	2	6,032	20,182	26,214
8	Persons serving about churches, etc.......	13,907	196	14,103	47,594	61,697
9	Teachers and educators..................	33,609	1,664	35,273	90,241	125,514
10	Science, literature, and art	2,704	166	2,870	5,252	8,122
11	Medical and sanitary work...............	6,854	2,916	9,770	16,415	26,185
12	Service for charitable organizations.......	163	34	197	432	629
13	Personal and domestic service...........	61,992	113,740	175,732	159,105	334,837
14	Living on income from capital or supported by relatives..................	33,346	25,074	58,420	113,485	171,905
15	Supported by the treasury or by charitable institutions.....................	11,371	8,765	20,136	5,998	26,134
16	Prisoners and convicts...................	3,907	414	4,321	102	4,423
17	Agriculture............................	29,047	4,054	33,101	130,925	164,026
18	Agriculture and sericulture..............	61	5	66	119	185
19	Cattle raising, etc....:.................	1,789	305	2,094	5,031	7,125
20	Forestry and forest industries............	3,291	89	3,380	9,496	12,876
21	Fishing and hunting....................	1,955	15	1,970	6,539	8,509
22	Mining................................	1,331	50	1,381	3,873	5,254
23	Metal smelting.........................	37	....	37	92	129
24	Manufactures of animal products..........	20,771	705	21,476	50,744	72,220
25	Manufactures of wood...................	41,506	1,019	42,525	96,951	139,476
26	Textile industry.......................	21,454	13,158	34,612	58,686	93,298
27	Manufactures of metal..................	42,828	621	43,449	104,880	148,329
28	Pottery and ceramic industry............	5,017	341	5,358	15,333	20,691

TOTAL JEWISH POPULATION AND NUMBER ENGAGED IN GAINFUL OCCUPATIONS,
BY OCCUPATIONS, 1897—Concluded.

Class No.	Occupation.	Persons engaged in gainful occupations.			Members of their families.	Total.
		Male.	Female.	Total.		
29	Chemical industry	5,137	1,843	6,980	13,742	20,722
30	Production of spirituous liquors	3,972	116	4,088	12,225	16,313
31	Production of other beverages	2,239	255	2,494	7,170	9,664
32	Production of foods, animal and vegetable	38,713	7,443	46,156	137,160	183,316
33	Tobacco, and tobacco manufactures	4,432	3,424	7,856	9,690	17,546
34	Printing and paper industries	13,487	2,222	15,709	25,804	41,513
35	Scientific instruments, watches, and toys	7,143	73	7,216	14,245	21,461
36	Jewelry, painting, articles of luxury, etc	6,349	162	6,511	12,026	18,537
37	Manufacture of clothing	202,714	51,670	254,384	528,070	782,454
38	Building industry	38,847	172	39,019	113,659	152,678
39	Carriage and wooden ship making	245	5	250	723	973
40	All other persons employed in manufacturing industry (manufacturers, clerical employees, etc.)	2,588	474	3,062	5,967	9,029
41	Transportation by water	2,020	30	2,050	7,702	9,752
42	Railroad employees	1,807	49	1,856	5,128	6,984
43	Carting and draying	38,050	337	38,387	132,337	170,724
44	All other means of communication and transportation	3,293	32	3,325	9,379	12,704
45	Post, telegraph, and telephone	310	16	326	818	1,144
46	Institutions of credit and insurance	2,299	109	2,408	5,376	7,784
47	Commercial middlemen	15,423	552	15,975	53,581	69,556
48	General commerce	80,637	15,578	96,215	302,722	398,937
49	Cattle trading	15,745	172	15,917	62,669	78,586
50	Trading in grain	46,483	2,480	48,963	172,624	221,587
51	Trading in all other agricultural products	115,343	29,716	145,059	442,048	587,107
52	Trading in structural material and in fuel	27,051	662	27,713	94,094	121,807
53	Trading in various goods for domestic use	4,810	1,043	5,853	15,967	21,820
54	Trading in metal goods, machinery, and arms	6,298	551	6,849	20,899	27,748
55	Trading in textiles and clothing	38,470	5,713	44,183	114,700	158,883
56	Trading in furs, leather, etc	11,774	777	12,551	42,153	54,704
57	Trading in articles of luxury, science, arts, etc	2,776	289	3,065	7,695	10,760
58	Trading in other goods	6,953	619	7,572	19,979	27,551
59	Peddlers and hucksters	14,812	5,058	19,870	49,850	69,720
60	Hotel and restaurant keepers	8,534	1,970	10,504	32,682	43,186
61	Dealers in spirituous liquors	10,802	1,334	12,136	44,440	56,576
62	Cleanliness and hygiene	5,489	3,508	8,997	18,237	27,234
63	Indefinite occupations	12,276	4,430	16,706	25,770	42,476
64	Prostitutes	128	1,148	1,276	488	1,764
65	Occupations unknown	7,484	7,943	15,427	16,037	31,464
	Total	1,204,937	325,370	1,530,307	3,532,849	5,063,156

For a concise and clear statement of the main facts of this table it has been thought desirable to prepare a table that will be, as far as possible, comparable with the occupation grouping of the United States census. For this purpose it was necessary to eliminate several classes that are omitted in United States occupation statistics, namely, class 14, "living on income from capital, or supported by relatives;" class 15, "supported by the treasury or by private charitable institutions;" class 16, "prisoners and convicts;" class 64, "prostitutes;" and class 65, "occupations unknown."

The one deviation from the United States system permitted is the distinction between those occupied in commerce and those in transportation.

With these modifications the distribution of the Russian Jews into the main occupation groups is as follows:

NUMBER AND PER CENT OF JEWS IN THE RUSSIAN EMPIRE ENGAGED IN EACH GROUP OF GAINFUL OCCUPATIONS, BY SEX, 1897.

[Compiled from Premier Recensement Général de la Population de l'Empire de Russie, 1897.]

Class Nos.	Group of occupations.	Males.	Per cent.	Females.	Per cent.	Total.	Per cent.
17–21	Agricultural pursuits	36,143	3.1	4,468	1.6	40,611	2.9
1–3,5–11	Professional service	66,944	5.8	5,006	1.8	71,950	5.0
4,12,13, 60–63	}Personal service(a)	152,450	13.3	125,016	44.3	277,466	19.4
22–40	Manufacturing and mechanical pursuits.	458,810	39.9	83,753	29.7	542,563	37.9
41–45	Transportation	45,480	4.0	464	.2	45,944	3.2
46–59	Commercial pursuits(a)	388,874	33.9	63,319	22.4	452,193	31.6
	Total	1,148,701	100.0	282,026	100.0	1,430,727	100.0

a In order to make figures comparable with figures in the United States census, hotel, restaurant, and saloon keepers are included in personal service.

In view of the theory generally accepted both in Russia and in the United States that the European Jew is in the majority of cases a merchant and only in America is transformed into a productive worker, it is important to emphasize the fact that of those who were employed in 1897 only one-third of the males and less than one-fourth of the females were occupied in commercial undertakings, or only 31.6 per cent of all the Jews employed, while the manufacturing and mechanical pursuits claimed almost two-fifths of those engaged in gainful occupations.

The small number of Jews engaged in agriculture is clearly brought out in the table. The economic function of the Jewish population of Russia may be further elucidated by a comparison of the occupation statistics of the Jews with those of the non-Jewish population of Russia.

NUMBER AND PER CENT OF JEWS AND OF OTHER PERSONS IN THE RUSSIAN EMPIRE ENGAGED IN EACH GROUP OF GAINFUL OCCUPATIONS, 1897.

[Compiled from Premier Recensement Général de la Population de l'Empire de Russie, 1897.]

Group of occupations.	Persons other than Jews.	Per cent.	Jews.	Per cent.
Agricultural pursuits	18,204,676	60.5	40,611	2.9
Professional service	916,863	3.0	71,950	5.0
Personal service(a)	4,872,546	16.2	277,466	19.4
Manufacturing and mechanical pursuits	4,627,356	15.4	542,563	37.9
Transportation	668,801	2.2	45,944	3.2
Commerce(a)	804,137	2.7	452,193	31.6
Total	30,094,379	100.0	1,430,727	100.0

a In order to make figures comparable with figures in the United States census, hotel, restaurant, and saloon keepers are included in personal service.

According to this table, 60.5 per cent of the non-Jewish population in gainful occupations in Russia were engaged in agriculture, while of the Jews 2.9 per cent were so employed. Of persons other than Jews only 2.7 per cent were engaged in commerce, while 31.6 per cent of the Jews were so engaged. The proportion of Jews in manufacturing and mechanical pursuits was nearly two and a half times as great as that of persons other than Jews employed in those pursuits. Although the Jews constitute only a little over 4 per cent of the entire Russian population, the number of Jews employed in manufacturing and mechanical pursuits is 10.5 per cent of the total population so engaged and the Jews engaged in commerce represent 36 per cent of the whole commercial class. The table shows, however, that the entire commercial class in Russia constitutes only 4 per cent and the Jews engaged in commerce only 1.4 per cent of the total number of persons in gainful occupations in Russia.

Since the Jews occupy but a small portion of the vast Empire, a comparison limited to that portion seems to promise more practical results.

NUMBER AND PER CENT OF JEWS AND OF OTHER PERSONS IN THE PALE ENGAGED IN EACH GROUP OF GAINFUL OCCUPATIONS, 1897.

[Compiled from Premier Recensement Général de la Population de l'Empire de Russie, 1897.]

Group of occupations.	Total employed.	Per cent.	Jews.	Per cent.	Persons other than Jews.	Per cent.
Agricultural pursuits	6,071,413	55.9	38,538	2.9	6,032,875	63.2
Professional service	317,710	2.9	67,238	5.1	250,472	2.6
Personal service (a)	2,139,981	19.7	250,078	18.8	1,889,903	19.8
Manufacturing and mechanical pursuits	1,573,519	14.4	504,844	37.9	1,068,675	11.2
Transportation	211,983	2.0	44,177	3.3	167,806	1.8
Commerce (a)	556,086	5.1	426,628	32.0	129,458	1.4
Total	10,870,692	100.0	1,331,503	100.0	9,539,189	100.0

a In order to make figures comparable with figures in the United States census, hotel, restaurant, and saloon keepers are included in personal service; hence the totals for commerce in this table do not agree with those given in the tables on pages 554 and 556.

With a commercial class that amounts to only 5.1 per cent of the working population of the Pale, the claim of the overcrowding of that class would hardly seem justified, and the Jews inhabiting the large cities naturally fill this class. Within the Pale the Jews employed in commerce constitute more than four-fifths of all persons so employed, and in the industrial class (manufacturing and mechanical pursuits) more than one-third.

In reality the contrast between the number of Jews employed in the various groups of occupations and the number of persons other than Jews employed in the same groups is still stronger than these tables indicate, because of the peculiarities of the Russian occupation statistics. In the class of persons employed all persons actually working are not reported, but only the "self-dependent" ones. Thus, of a large agricultural family, containing from three to six adult workers, only one person—the head of the family—is reported as "employed in family," while in the United States census all persons occupied in farm work would be so reported. If the children and dependents are added, the agricultural class swells considerably, and the percentage of the commercial class is correspondingly reduced.

An analysis of the statistics of the occupations of the Jews by separate regions shows that, while there is a general uniformity, there are characteristic differences in the distribution, especially in the comparative proportions of the industrial and commercial classes. In the northwest, namely, in Lithuania and in White Russia, the industrial occupations claim a much greater proportion of the employed than commerce (44.2 per cent against 23.8 per cent and 42.2 per cent against 27.4 per cent, respectively). This difference is significant in view of the greater congestion of the Jews in the northwest and their lower economic condition, as will be indicated in another section. It will be shown that in these Provinces there is a process of rapid shifting from the commercial pursuits to industrial work, and here also the labor movement is strongest. It is from these Provinces that until very recently emigration to the United States was strongest. The following table shows the distribution of Jews in the various occupation groups for each region of the Pale and for Russia outside of the Pale:

NUMBER AND PER CENT OF JEWS IN EACH GROUP OF GAINFUL OCCUPATIONS IN THE PALE, BY REGIONS, AND IN RUSSIA OUTSIDE OF THE PALE, 1897.

[Compiled from the separate reports on Provinces of Premier Recensement Général de la Population de l'Empire de Russie, 1897.]

Groups of gainful occupations.	Lithuania.		White Russia.		Southwestern Russia.		Southern (new) Russia.	
	Number.	Per cent.	Number.	Per cent.	Number.	Per cent.	Number.	Per cent.
Agricultural pursuits	8,279	4.0	8,223	4.2	6,427	1.7	9,614	4.5
Professional service	10,455	5.1	11,556	5.8	21,226	5.6	10,571	4.9
Personal service(a)	38,819	19.0	31,865	16.1	62,112	16.5	37,473	17.5
Manufacturing and mechanical pursuits	90,322	44.2	83,656	42.2	132,787	35.3	74,361	34.7
Transportation	8,053	3.9	8,507	4.3	11,481	3.1	6,202	2.9
Commerce(a)	48,608	23.8	54,359	27.4	142,368	37.8	76,151	35.5
Total	204,536	100.0	198,166	100.0	376,401	100.0	214,372	100.0

Groups of gainful occupations.	Poland.		Pale.		Russia outside of Pale.		Russian Empire.	
	Number.	Per cent.	Number.	Per cent.	Number.	Per cent.	Number.	Per cent.
Agricultural pursuits	5,995	1.8	38,538	2.9	2,073	2.1	40,611	2.9
Professional service	13,430	4.0	67,238	5.1	4,712	4.7	71,950	5.0
Personal service(a)	79,809	23.6	250,078	18.8	27,388	27.6	277,466	19.4
Manufacturing and mechanical pursuits	123,718	36.6	504,844	37.9	37,719	38.0	542,563	37.9
Transportation	9,934	2.9	44,177	3.3	1,767	1.8	45,944	3.2
Commerce(a)	105,142	31.1	b 426,628	32.0	25,565	26.8	452,193	31.6
Total	338,028	100.0	1,331,503	100.0	99,224	100.0	1,430,727	100.0

a In order to make figures comparable with figures in the United States census, hotel, restaurant and saloon keepers are included in personal service.
b This total does not agree with that shown in the tables on pages 554 and 556 for the reason stated in note a.

In this connection it is interesting to determine from which of the occupation groups the largest part of the Russian-Jewish immigrants in the United States is drawn. This not only has a practical bearing upon the American problem of immigration, but also is of importance from the Russian point of view as a method of determining the effect of this emigration upon the economic make-up of the Jewish Pale in Russia. Up to 1898 the reports of the United States Commissioner of Immigration have given the statistics of occupation by countries of origin, and since then by nationality. Neither method is altogether satisfactory when the occupations of the Russian Jews are to be determined. But as the Jewish immigrants from Russia during the six years 1901-1906 constituted 71.9 per cent of all the Jewish immigrants, the figures showing the occupations of all the Jews who came into the United States during that period are at least suggestive of the occupations of the Russian Jews:

NUMBER OF JEWS ARRIVING IN THE UNITED STATES DURING EACH OF THE YEARS ENDING JUNE 30, 1901 to 1906, BY OCCUPATIONS.

[From Annual Reports of the Commissioner-General of Immigration.]

Occupation.	1901.	1902.	1903.	1904.	1905.	1906.
Professions:						
Actors..	20	4	16	28	25	23
Clergy..	5	14	27	51	57	52
Editors...	2	3	4	13	23	10
Engineers and electricians......................	30	38	81	98	123	116
Lawyers..	2	1	2	6	7	3
Musicians......................................	61	52	108	260	342	227
Physicians.....................................	12	6	9	70	94	40
Sculptors and artists..........................	16	25	31	36	47	43
Teachers.......................................	103	98	147	211	322	333
Not specified..................................	43	38	74	70	123	247
Total......................................	294	279	499	843	1,163	1,094
Skilled trades:						
Bakers...	627	592	937	1,173	1,460	1,102
Barbers and hairdressers.......................	164	172	266	403	578	594
Blacksmiths....................................	519	434	695	826	1,568	840
Bookbinders....................................				535	705	587
Brewers..	10	14	14	19	32	37
Butchers.......................................	525	591	743	1,401	2,036	1,237
Cabinetmakers, carpenters, etc.................	1,874	2,018	2,600	4,632	6,289	5,462
Clerks, accountants, etc.......................	618	549	1,060	1,838	2,512	2,288
Engineers and firemen..........................				84	110	77
Engravers......................................	22	14	23	20	40	48
Furriers.......................................				410	620	530
Gardeners......................................	17	17	19	26	43	38
Hat and cap makers.............................				683	1,009	718
Ironworkers....................................	8	26	22	148	95	75
Jewelers.......................................	152	170	193	179	193	181
Locksmiths.....................................	315	315	691	1,337	1,589	1,314
Machinists.....................................	142	96	166	254	366	193
Mariners.......................................	33	14	13	71	52	75
Masons...	75	111	153	296	469	431
Mechanics (not specified)......................	149	84	159	108	129	121
Metal workers (other than iron, steel, or tin)....				419	559	463
Millers..	88	62	85	140	211	138
Milliners......................................				101	273	488
Miners...	19	12	13	19	15	45
Painters and glaziers..........................	799	808	1,131	1,970	2,849	2,297
Photographers..................................				145	214	219
Plasterers.....................................	1	1	5	14	11	17
Plumbers.......................................	18	16	39	59	93	77
Printers.......................................	91	91	154	303	387	393
Saddlers and harness makers....................	104	109	206	281	358	256
Seamstresses and dressmakers...................	1,811	1,704	3,315	3,814	3,657	5,845
Shipwrights....................................	2					1

NUMBER OF JEWS ARRIVING IN THE UNITHD STATES DURING EACH OF THE
YEARS ENDING JUNE 30, 1901 TO 1906, BY OCCUPATIONS—Concluded.

Occupation.	1901.	1902.	1903.	1904.	1905.	1906.
Skilled trades—Concluded.						
Shoemakers	1,284	1,285	1,614	2,763	3,824	2,353
Stonecutters	10	12	21	24	32	21
Tailors	5,981	6,110	9,233	16,426	22,334	18,418
Tanners and curriers	341	270	497	347	531	254
Tinners	427	517	727	882	1,016	832
Tobacco manufacturers	297	232	346	532	651	560
Upholsterers				229	253	228
Watch and clock makers	249	196	233	561	667	720
Weavers and spinners and other textile workers.	172	127	287	481	963	620
Wheelwrights	9	19	31	28	74	51
Woodworkers				271	283	213
Not specified	1,399	1,053	1,280	857	985	744
Total	18,352	17,841	27,071	45,109	60,135	51,141
Miscellaneous:						
Agents	8	4	6	26	31	82
Bankers			1	7	5	10
Draymen, hackmen, etc				33	61	44
Farmers	78	58	46	65	122	168
Farm laborers	301	317	334	296	498	1,712
Hotel keepers	18	11	20	18	24	29
Laborers	3,906	5,316	6,664	8,371	8,159	8,378
Manufacturers				74	90	47
Merchants	1,999	2,246	2,363	3.464	4,596	3,495
Servants	889	5,122	7,039	9,292	8,000	9,839
Not specified	546	542	1,008	153	155	566
Total	7,745	13,616	17,481	21,799	21,741	24,370
No occupation	31,707	25,952	31,152	38,485	46,871	77,143
Total Hebrew immigrants	58,098	57,688	76,203	106,236	129,910	153,748

It appears that 63.0 per cent of the Jewish immigrants during
the period 1901 to 1906 who were fit to pursue a gainful occupation
belong to the class of industrial workers, and undoubtedly a large
proportion of the common laborers classified with personal service
(according to the scheme followed by the United States census) are
in reality industrial workers.

In the following table the occupations in the preceding table have
been grouped in accordance with the scheme of the Twelfth Census
of the United States:

NUMBER AND PER CENT OF JEWISH IMMIGRANTS TO THE UNITED STATES ENGAGED
IN EACH GROUP OF OCCUPATIONS FOR THE PERIOD 1901 TO 1906.

[Compiled from data presented in Annual Reports of the Commissioner-General of Immigration.]

Group of occupations.	Number.	Per cent.
Agricultural pursuits	4,155	1.3
Professional service	4,172	1.3
Domestic and personal service	83,272	25.2
Trade and transportation	27,557	8.3
Manufacturing and mechanical pursuits	208,447	63.0
Miscellaneous	2,970	.9
Total	330,573	100.0

The statement has often been made that in the United States the
Russian Jew has for the first time learned manual labor. The statistics of the occupations in Russia, as well as those of the United

States Bureau of Immigration, show that such a statement is not warranted. While the point of religion has not been touched upon, a study of the data presented in the Twelfth Census of the United States relative to the occupation of the Russian Jews in New York City shows that skilled and unskilled labor predominate in the various means employed by these Jews in order to earn a livelihood. A great deal of statistical information in regard to the Russian Jews in New York City may be obtained from the report on "Occupations," since in that report the persons employed in gainful occupations are classified by nativity. As the natives of Finland, Russia, and Poland entering the United States are separately reported, and as immigration of other nationalities from Russia has been very small until recently, and since few Lithuanians and Germans who arrive from Russia remain in New York City, the groups of persons in New York City designated as natives of Russia may be taken as equivalent to the Jews.

The following table shows the per cent of all nationalities and of Russians in New York City engaged in each group of gainful occupations in 1900:

PER CENT OF ALL NATIONALITIES AND OF RUSSIANS IN NEW YORK CITY ENGAGED
IN EACH GROUP OF OCCUPATIONS, BY SEX, 1900.

[Compiled from data presented in Report on Occupations, Twelfth Census of the United States, 1900.]

Group of occupations.	Males.		Females.		Total.	
	All nationalities.	Russians.	All nationalities.	Russians.	All nationalities.	Russians.
Agricultural pursuits	0.9	0.3	0.1	0.2	0.7	0.3
Professional service	5.5	3.0	6.1	1.5	5.7	2.7
Domestic and personal service	18.7	5.1	39.9	12.5	24.0	6.7
Trade and transportation	36.8	30.5	17.8	14.5	32.0	27.0
Manufacturing and mechanical pursuits	38.1	61.1	36.1	71.3	37.6	63.3
Total	100.0	100.0	100.0	100.0	100.0	100.0

The difference becomes still greater when the percentage of Russians is compared not with that of the entire working population, but with the percentage of all the other elements of the New York City population engaged in gainful occupations:

PER CENT OF RUSSIANS AND OF ALL OTHER NATIONALITIES IN NEW YORK CITY
ENGAGED IN EACH GROUP OF OCCUPATIONS, 1900.

[Compiled from data presented in Report on Occupations, Twelfth Census of the United States, 1900.]

Group of occupations.	Russians.	All other nationalities.
Agricultural pursuits	0.3	0.7
Professional service	2.7	5.9
Domestic and personal service	6.7	25.2
Trade and transportation	27.0	32.4
Manufacturing and mechanical pursuits	63.3	35.8
Total	100.0	100.0

The claim has also been made that the choice of occupations is primarily a question of national predilection, and from this point of view the tendency of the Russian Jew to go into trade has been usually judged. While it has been shown above how greatly exaggerated this supposed tendency is, the data in regard to the occupations of the Russian Jews in New York City seem to furnish strong evidence that economic conditions, such as opportunities and local demand, have a much more decisive influence than mere national predilection, and that even the latter may be nothing more than the result of the accumulated effect of economic conditions, such as have forced the Russian Jew into commercial pursuits and have often kept him there even after those pursuits have ceased to be profitable. Yet the rapid shifting of the Jew into mechanical industry both in Russia and in this country indicates that the influence of these historic conditions can not be as strong as is generally believed.

Another noteworthy feature revealed by the United States census is the characteristic dislike of the Russian Jew, and still more of the Jewess, to enter domestic service. While a great number of domestic servants register at the immigration stations, most of them seem to drift rapidly into other occupations, preferring the more onerous but more independent existence of an industrial workingman or working-woman to that of a household servant.

AGRICULTURE.

AGRICULTURAL COLONIES.

Numerically, the farmers do not represent a very considerable proportion of the Jewish race in Russia; but in view of the almost universal conviction that the Jewish character is incompatible with agricultural pursuits, it will be a revelation to many Americans to learn that there are more than 40,000 Jews in Russia who are independently employed in farming and that more than 150,000 persons are supported by them, so that altogether over 190,000 persons of Jewish faith derive their subsistence from agricultural pursuits. This fact makes the data in regard to Jewish agriculture not only interesting, but of practical importance to the people of the United States. The condition of the Jewish farmers in Russia has been the subject of many thorough investigations, the most recent and exhaustive being that made by the St. Petersburg committee of the Jewish Colonization Society. The data for this investigation were gathered by a house-to-house canvass at the end of the last century and the results were published in 1904. This source will be mainly relied upon for statistical information as to agricultural conditions.

When Russia, by the annexation of a portion of Poland, acquired authority over a large Jewish population, the Jews represented the commercial and the industrial classes of Poland. During the first half of the nineteenth century the acknowledged effort of the Russian Government was to break up Jewish exclusiveness and encourage the assimilation of the Jews with the Russian people.

A part of this policy was the effort to attract Jews to agricultural pursuits, and to this end purchase and rental of land by Jews were encouraged by Alexander I and by Nicholas I. During the reign of the former the law of December 9, 1804, was passed, a law which not only permitted the settlement and the buying of land by Jews in new Russia, but created a fund for the settlement of Jews in agricultural colonies in that sparsely settled part of the Empire. Special inducements also were offered to Jewish colonists, as, for instance, freedom from military service for twenty-five and even fifty years. Several colonies were established, and by 1810 about 1,700 Jewish families were settled on the lands of the Province of Kherson.

In that year the transfer of Jews to new Russia was discontinued because of the exhaustion of the funds assigned. In 1823 a grant of 50,000 rubles made possible the further settlement of about 500 Jewish families.

This concluded the experiments of colonizing new Russia with Jews during the reign of Alexander I. During the reign of his successor, Nicholas I, similar efforts, assisted by private benevolence, were directed toward voluntary settlement of Jews in country districts, and in the forties, in accordance with the provisions of the law of April 13 (25), 1835, several colonies were established in the Provinces of Kherson and Yekaterinoslav. These efforts, at least as far as new Russia was concerned, were discontinued in 1865. The experiment of sending Jewish would-be agriculturists to Siberia, which was undertaken in 1835, was abandoned in the following year. In new Russia the number of colonies grew from 15 in 1847 to 371 in 1865. The law of 1835 was also operative in the western Provinces, but the condition of the soil and the life of agricultural classes in that region were not such as to attract the Jews. In 1859 the settlement of Jews on Government lands in the western region was stopped, and in 1864 the colonizing of Jews on private lands was prohibited.

The attitude of the Government toward the question of colonizing Jews and attracting them to an agricultural life has evidently changed. The reason usually given for this change was the small attendant success. When the radical nature of the experiment is considered, it seems evident that the process could not prove immediately successful. The evidences of the desire to engage in agricultural pursuits were many, and toward the second half of the nineteenth century a general decline of the prosperity of the urban Jew, caused by the Polish insurrection, created the proper conditions for Jewish land settlement, but unfortunately the attitude of the Government had changed. Finally, the May laws of 1882, while they did not affect the colonies as such, put an end to the application of Jewish private enterprise and capital to land ownership and farming, which had been making rapid strides contemporaneously with, but independently of, the colonies. These laws prohibited the Jews from buying or renting lands outside of the limits of the cities and incorporated towns (the so-called "miestechkos.") These temporary rules, which extended to the 15 Provinces of western Russia, exclusive of Poland, were never repealed, and in 1891 the Jews were prohibited from buying or renting land from the peasants in Poland.

The size of the homestead is one of the main factors in the economic situation of a farmer. The standard of agricultural technique prevailing in Russia makes intensive agriculture almost an impossibility and demands a large farm. A hundred years ago agricultural methods in Russia were still more primitive than they are now, and it was hardly to be expected that the Jew, as a beginner in agriculture, would immediately excel his Russian neighbor in the methods of tilling the soil. In the Province of Kherson, where nearly 25 per cent of all the Jewish "colonists" are located, and where on the whole they have been most successful, the original "colonists" were granted homesteads of 30 dessiatines (81.06 acres), but the increase of population, division of households, etc., have considerably decreased the size of the land holdings of the farmers. In the western region the average size of a lot on which the Jewish colonist started his agricultural career was still smaller, usually about 20 dessiatines (54.04 acres).

The following table shows the total number of Jewish colonies, the number of Jewish peasant families, and the area of land in their possession:

NUMBER OF JEWISH COLONIES, HOUSEHOLDS, AND MEMBERS, AND ACRES HELD BY THE COLONISTS, BY REGIONS, 1898.

Region.	Number of colonies.	Households.		Number of acres.
		Number.	Members.	
Northwestern Provinces	188	2,731	18,504	66,012.5
Southwestern Provinces	60	2,227	12,155	31,975.5
Southern (new) Russia	48	5,592	32,683	171,390.6
Poland	(a)	2,509	12,545	36,028.5
Total	b 296	13,059	75,887	305,407.1

a Not reported.   b Not including colonists in Poland not reported.

In new Russia the average holding per household is 11.34 dessiatines (30.6 acres), while in the northwestern Provinces the average farm is but 8.95 dessiatines (24.2 acres), although the quality of the land is much inferior to that of the black soil of new Russia. In the southwestern Provinces, as well as in Poland, the average size of a farm is only 5.31 dessiatines (14.3 acres). The average farm of the Jewish peasant, therefore, contains no more than 8.66 dessiatines (23.4 acres).

Of all the experiments to turn the Jew to an agricultural life the colonies established in the Province of Kherson were placed under the most favorable conditions and gave the best results. These colonies deserve, therefore, detailed description. The colonies were started with an allotment from the Government of 30 dessiatines (81.06 acres) for each family, but under the influence of varying conditions this equality did not persist very long. There began in the Jewish colonies the same process of differentiation that is characteristic of the entire Russian peasantry, so that only a portion of the colonists' households are provided with sufficient land to make a practical success of farming. This is clearly shown in the following table:

NUMBER AND PER CENT OF JEWISH HOUSEHOLDS AND OF ACRES OWNED, AND AVERAGE SIZE OF HOLDING, IN THE COLONIES OF KHERSON, BY GROUPS OF HOUSEHOLDS, 1898.

Households owning—	Households.		Acres owned.		Average holding (acres).
	Number.	Per cent.	Number.	Per cent.	
No land...	611	19.2	....	....	....
Less than 13.5 acres..............................	483	15.2	4,923	5.1	10.2
13.5 to 27 acres...................................	836	26.2	19,172	19.8	22.9
27 to 54 acres.....................................	728	22.8	30,069	31.0	41.3
54 acres or over...................................	529	16.6	42,846	44.1	81.0
Total...	3,187	100.0	97,010	100.0	30.4

Only one-sixth of the households own at present 54 acres or more per family, and this one-sixth owns 44.1 per cent of the entire land of the colonies. Many of the farmers have extended their activity by renting, since 1,165 households were found to rent additional land, the total area rented in 1898 amounting to 25,203¼ dessiatines (68,099.2 acres). On the other hand, 811 households let out a part or the whole of their holdings, the total area let out amounting to but 7,524½ dessiatines (20,331.2 acres). If the amount let out is subtracted from the amount rented there is shown a net increase in holdings due to rentals of 17,678¾ dessiatines (47,768.0 acres), or an average for the 3,187 households of 5.5 dessiatines (14.9 acres).

The following table shows the effect of the renting of land upon the average size of the farming establishments:

AVERAGE SIZE OF ALLOTMENTS OWNED, AVERAGE NET INCREASE DUE TO RENTALS, AND AVERAGE SIZE OF TOTAL HOLDINGS IN THE COLONIES OF KHERSON, BY GROUPS OF HOUSEHOLDS, 1898.

[The "average net increase due to rentals" is the excess of the amount of land rented over the amount let out.]

Households owning—	Average size of allotment owned (acres).	Average net increase due to rentals (acres).	Average total holdings (acres).
No land		25.7	25.7
Less than 13.5 acres	10.2	22.4	32.6
13.5 to 27 acres	22.9	20.0	42.9
27 to 54 acres	41.3	8.6	49.9
54 acres or over	81.0	a 3.5	77.5
Total	30.4	14.9	45.3

a Excess of land let out over land rented.

Agricultural pursuits are not congenial to all colonists in the same degree. While there are undoubtedly many who prefer to lease their comparatively large holdings, which they are prohibited by law from selling, there is a sufficient number of others who are anxious to apply their labor to farming on rented land.

If the condition of the surrounding Russian peasantry be taken as a basis of comparison, these Jewish peasants are fairly well provided with working live stock, the average number of horses per family being 2.28. Yet there are 1,018 households that do not possess any horses at all, and 216 that possess only one horse each, so that only 1,953 or 61.3 per cent of the households own two horses or more.

In the character of their agricultural methods, the kind of implements they use, and the crops they grow, the Jewish peasants of these colonies of the Province of Kherson differ little from their Russian neighbors, from whom they received their first lessons in agriculture. Like the Russian peasants, the Jews plant more than two-thirds of their land in cereals, the rest being left for grazing purposes; but grass sowing is almost unknown. The climate of Kherson is well fitted for spring crops, and the colonists plant more than four-fifths of their cultivated land in spring wheat, barley, and other spring cereals; and practically all the rest in winter cereals. According to a comparison made in 1898 by the statistician of the Province of Kherson, the Jewish colonists planted in cereals 98.3 per cent of their land under cultivation; the Russian peasants of the same district, 96.4 per cent; the Bulgarian peasants, of whom a number live in the same Province, 99.9 per cent, and the German colonists, 92.4 per cent.

From the implements these farmers use may be judged the primitive methods of tilling the soil. Sixty-three per cent of the households did not own any implements for plowing the ground and had to borrow them for temporary use. In all the colonies of Kherson there were found only 632 plows, and 1,137 so-called "bukkers," peculiar plowing implements of southern Russia which scarcely do more than scratch the soil. Almost 80 per cent of the land under cultivation had been plowed with these "bukkers," and only 20 per cent with regular steel plows. The extremely short time during which the harvest must be gathered in southern Russia made the introduction of harvesting machines an absolute necessity. The thrashing is still done in the most primitive fashion. The harvested grain is spread over a suitable piece of ground and horses harnessed to iron rollers are driven over the straw, the horses' hoofs cooperating with the heavy metal rollers in separating the seed from the straw.

The returns from agriculture can not be very great, when such methods are used. According to official statistics the average yield of cereals in the Province of Kherson in 1898 was as follows:

	Bushels per acre.
On private estates	9.9
On lands of German colonists	9.1
On lands of Bulgarians	7.6
On lands of Jewish colonists	7.5
On lands of Russian peasants	6.8

According to these figures the Jews show better results than the Russian peasants, whose only occupation for many centuries was agriculture.

Whatever the returns, it is important to know that the majority of the colonists make use only of their own labor in tilling their land. Very few colonists, mainly those whose possessions are considerably above the average, employ hired labor all the year round. The number of such households is only 210, or 6.6 per cent of the total, and the average number of laborers employed per household is 1.82. The number of families that are forced to hire additional labor during the season of plowing, or more especially, of harvesting and thrashing, is considerably greater, namely, 686, or 21.5 per cent; but many families who also hire permanent laborers are here included. The total number of households employing hired labor, whether permanently or temporarily, is only 704, or 22.1 per cent of all households.

Even if the rental value of land be disregarded, it can not be claimed that the reward of the labor of practically all the members of the family is considerable. By a careful calculation, based upon the average yield of the land and the price of cereals, the average annual income of a household has been estimated at 139 rubles ($71.59) from grain farming, and with the addition of the products of live stock (dairying and slaughtering), at 200 rubles ($103). In discussing this estimate an investigator says: (a)

Such an income would scarcely be sufficient for a family of a Russian peasant, who needs about 35 rubles ($18.03) per capita for his bare subsistence, according to the investigations of the well-known Russian statistician, Mr. Shcherbina. But the standard of a Jewish family is evidently higher. The Jewish population of the colonies has kept certain civilized customs, which they find difficult to give up; thus they do not spare expenses for teaching their children; they are accustomed to better food, and they dress better on holidays, and have considerable expenses for religious purposes, for medical treatment, etc. From data in regard to the budgets of five agricultural Jewish families in the Province of Vilna, it appears that the normal budget of a Jewish family is not less than 300 rubles ($154.50). Persons well acquainted with the life of the southern colonists estimate the normal expenditures of a family at the same figure. No matter how approximate our calculations, one may assert with a reasonable degree of certainty that the income from agriculture does not by far correspond to the needs of the population of the colonies, and that subsidiary occupations therefore are a necessity for some part of the families.

Facts seem to support this reasoning, for a considerable number of the families in the colonies have been forced to look for additional sources of income. Of the 3,187 families living in the Kherson colonies, only 1,563, or 49.0 per cent, have no other occupation but agriculture; 1,194 families, or 37.5 per cent, have an additional occupation, and 430 families, or 13.5 per cent, have abandoned agriculture and have devoted themselves to other occupations. The proportion of the latter is not great enough to support the claim that the Jewish colonists have proved unwilling or unfit to be land tillers. At the same time, the possibilities of profitable employment at commerce and handicrafts for local demand, as well as the demand of the surrounding rural communities, have been utilized by some of the colonists. The amount of available labor in a family seems to have been the decisive factor in the combination of agriculture with other pursuits, for of the families without any adult workers only 21.5 per cent pursue at the same time other occupations than farming; of the families with one worker, 35.3 per cent, and of the families with more than one worker, 47.6 per cent. With the growth of population and the consequent reduction of the available land supply per household, this tendency to pursue other occupations must inevitably grow. A comparative statement is possible for one county (*uyezd*), the county of Elisabetgrad, where a similar investigation was made some fifteen years earlier. The proportion of households employed at agriculture alone decreased from 65.9 per cent to 47.9 per cent, while the

---

a See Sbornik Materialov ob Economicheskom Polozhenii Evreev v Rossii (Collection of material in regard to the economic condition of the Jews in Russia), Vol. I, page 40.

proportion of those who combined agricultural work with other pursuits increased from 24.8 per cent to 32.7 per cent, and the proportion of those who abandoned agriculture rose from 9.3 per cent to 19.4 per cent. These changes took place during the comparatively short period of fifteen years, from 1883–1885 to 1898–99. During the same period the population of the three colonies located in this "uyezd" increased more than 50 per cent, and the average supply of land per person decreased from 17.5 to 10.1 dessiatines (from 47.3 to 27.3 acres). In the neighboring Province of Yekaterinoslav seventeen colonies were established within the decade 1845–1855 and under conditions very similar to those in Kherson. The allotment of land was the same—i. e., 30 dessiatines (81.1 acres), except for two colonies, where it was 35 dessiatines (94.6 acres) and 40 dessiatines (108.1 acres), respectively. The average amount of land per family in 1897 was 12.5 dessiatines (33.8 acres), or about the same as in the Province of Kherson. In addition to the 17,650 dessiatines (47,690 acres) owned, 7,814 dessiatines (21,113 acres) were rented. A detailed investigation was made of these colonies in 1890, when their condition was described as fairly satisfactory. At that time 749 households were found, of which 524, or 70 per cent, tilled their land by their own labor; 93, or 12.4 per cent, made use of hired labor in addition to their own; 77, or 10.3 per cent, relied upon hired labor exclusively, and only 55 families, or 7.3 per cent, did not occupy themselves with agriculture at all. Like the colonists of Kherson, those of Yekaterinoslav grow cereals, preferably wheat, rye, and barley, to the exclusion of everything else.

In the realization of its object of attracting the Jews toward agriculture the Government pursued two lines of activity. The one consisted in settling the Jews in the sparsely populated lands of New Russia, the other in encouraging voluntary settlement of Jews on State or on private lands. In the latter case the land was either bought or rented. Although the Jewish colonies were entitled to a subsidy at the time of settling in their new homes, the land was usually so poor and the success of the Jewish farmers often so indifferent that many of the colonists were forced to leave their colonies and return to the towns. Nevertheless, the investigation undertaken by the agents of the Jewish Colonization Society in 1899 proved the existence of 248 Jewish agricultural settlements, containing a population of 4,958 families, or 30,659 persons. But the land at the disposal of these families is limited to 36,265 dessiatines (97,988 acres), which gives an average of 7.3 dessiatines (19.7 acres) per family, or 1.2 dessiatines (3.2 acres) per person. How insufficient this area is for grain farming may be judged from the fact that the average plot owned by the Jewish colonist is considerably smaller than the corresponding plot of his peasant neighbor.

Thus, in the six northwestern Provinces the average amount of arable land per each male person of the peasant class was 2.25 dessiatines (6.1 acres), while for the Jewish colonists the average was only 1.5 dessiatines (4.1 acres). In the four southwestern Provinces of Volhynia, Kiev, Podolia, and Chernigov the comparative areas were 1.75 and 0.7 dessiatines (4.7 and 1.9 acres). This insufficiency of land was mainly due to the activity of various commissions which redistributed the State lands in use by the peasants in the middle of the seventies, and reduced the allotments of the Jewish farmers on the plea that the land was not tilled by the labor of the colonists themselves. More than 33,000 dessiatines (89,166 acres) were taken from the Jewish colonists, and their land holdings reduced by more than 50 per cent. The prohibition against Jews buying land in the nine western Provinces, which dates back to 1864, and the laws of 1882, which prohibit the renting of land by Jews, prevented any compensation for this loss by purchase or by rental.

Under these conditions successful agriculture was hardly to be expected. Only a very small proportion of the farmers is provided with a sufficient area of land, 42.1 per cent of the colonists having less than 2.5 dessiatines (6.8 acres), 39.9 per cent from 2.5 to 10 dessiatines (6.8 to 27 acres), and only 18 per cent more than 10 dessiatines (27 acres). Only a little more than one-half of the colonists actually plow their own land, and the average surface cultivated by a family is equal to 4 dessiatines (10.8 acres) in the northwestern Provinces and only 2.5 dessiatines (6.8 acres) in the southwestern region. The methods and the implements, or rather their absence, are similar to those of the ignorant peasants of Lithuania or of White Russia, and practically all these "farmers" without land are forced to look to other fields for support. Thus only 13 per cent of the families devoted themselves entirely to agriculture. In addition to agriculture the handicrafts, commerce, and unskilled labor were the principal occupations of the colonists. The statement that if the families with less than 2.5 dessiatines (6.8 acres) be excluded three-fourths of the remaining families plow their land would seem to show that the utmost use is made of the land. Although the main colonies of Jewish land tillers are located in the Provinces of Kherson and Yekaterinoslav, numerous colonies, as well as individual land tillers, are scattered throughout the Jewish Pale, and even in Siberia may be found several villages inhabited by Jewish peasants. A few words may be added to show the condition of these peasants.

In Bessarabia nine colonies were established between 1836 and 1853, five of them on bought lands and four on lands acquired by rentals that run from twenty-five to fifty years. At the expiration of the contracts it was impossible to renew them in three out of these four colonies, and only six colonies exist at the present time. In many details these Bessarabian colonies differ from those already described. The enforced removal of Jews from villages has crowded into the colonies many families in no way connected with agricultural pursuits, and this has given to the colonies the appearance of commercial towns. Out of 1,500 families only 536 own land, and their average land holdings are but 5.48 dessiatines (14.8 acres), which is a great deal less than the average holdings in Kherson and also less than the average holdings of the peasants of this Province, 8.2 dessiatines (22.2 acres). On this land grain farming plays a small part, only 67 per cent of the land being under grain, the main cereal being maize. The colonies have a comparatively large grazing area, and several colonies keep large flocks of sheep for commercial purposes. Another distinctive feature of these colonies is a considerable development of various kinds of special crops, such as fruit, tobacco, and grapes. Not only in the colonies, but also in the Russian villages of the Province, do Jews occupy themselves with tobacco culture; in fact, almost all the tobacco growing in Bessarabia is done by Jews. The competition of the world's crop is gradually reducing the profits of this crop and is forcing the planters not provided with sufficient land for grain farming into viticulture. The results of this highly intensive crop are not very favorable, because of the primitive wine-making methods in use.

In Poland Jewish agriculture was encouraged mainly by grants of long periods of freedom from military service, and since that service before the introduction of the new military system lasted about twenty-five years the inducement was not inconsiderable. Though this privilege was withdrawn in 1864 many cases of settlement of Jews on farms occurred after that date, especially since the right of the Jew to acquire land remained unassailed in Poland longer than anywhere else in the Empire. Altogether 2,509 families of Jewish agriculturists, living either on separate farms or in small colonies, were found in Poland who held about 15,000 dessiatines (40,503 acres), or about 6 dessiatines (16 acres) per family.

The results of these experiments furnish sufficient material for a judgment of the social worth of these efforts. In so far as the simple question of the fitness of the Russian Jew for an agricultural career is concerned it seems to have been proved beyond doubt. Within a period of less than fifty years thousands of families have established themselves in rural communities, and tilling the land has been usually their main and often their only occupation. If their economic position is usually precarious, the same is true of the Russian peasant in general. The Jewish peasant suffers from the same cause as his neighbor—namely, an insufficiency of land—but suffers to a still greater degree. Both till their land with antiquated methods and inefficient implements. Both apply methods of extensive agriculture to a plot of land which, in view of its small dimensions, demands a

highly intensive cultivation.   It is small wonder that in either case
grain farming should lead to economic distress.   In addition to these
obstacles the Jew has to contend with a great many difficulties of a
legal nature, yet it is universally acknowledged that the physical
effects of the fifty years of farming have had an excellent influence
on the health and muscular development of the colonists.   The Jew
of Bessarabia, for instance, has none of the physical characteristics
that are supposed to be so typical of the Lithuanian Jew.   Had the
first benevolent efforts of the Government toward the introduction of
agriculture among the Jews been continued, agriculture might have
become an important occupation of the Jews, especially in view of
the many idealistic movements to return to the land which have
sprung up several times during the last 30 years, and caused the
organization of agricultural colonies of Russian Jews in many parts
of the world.

TRUCK FARMING.

It is still the custom in Russia to think of grain farming only when
speaking of farming, because of the very slight development of other
specialized forms of farming, or to use the inaccurate Russian expres-
sion, the cultivation of commercial crops.   Therefore the comparative popularity of these special branches of agriculture among Jews,
which the official occupation statistics fail to indicate, is the more
significant.

Through a private enumeration, which is far from being complete,
the following figures were obtained:

JEWS EMPLOYED IN SPECIAL BRANCHES OF AGRICULTURE, BY REGIONS AND KIND
OF FARMING, 1898.

Kind of farming.	Southern (new) Russia.	South-western Provinces.	North-western Provinces.	Poland.	Total.
Fruit growing	622	1,641	7,129	1,907	11,299
Tobacco culture	1,015	625	40	15	1,695
Viticulture	658	117		5	780
Other special farming	27	36		30	93
Total	2,322	2,419	7,169	1,957	13,867
Dairy farming	495	970	3,798	2,191	7,454
Apiculture	34	57	59	50	200
Total	2,851	3,446	11,026	4,198	21,521

In view of the many difficulties of acquiring land, these specialized
branches of farming that require only limited areas and a great outlay
of labor are most suitable for the Jews.   Altogether, the 13,867
farmers had at their disposal only 19,475 dessiatines (52,621 acres),
which gives an average of 1.4 dessiatines (3.8 acres) per farmer, and the
acquisition of even these small tracts of land was exceedingly difficult,
as the May laws of 1882 prohibit the sale or lease of land outside of

city limits to Jews. As a result, 7,714 dessiatines (20,843 acres), or nearly two-fifths of the entire land of these special farms, are within the city limits, and of the remaining 11,761 dessiatines (31,778 acres) only 1,336 dessiatines (3,610 acres) are the property of the farmers. Some renting of land to Jews outside the city limits continues notwithstanding the strict laws prohibiting it, but the insecure position of the tenant, who is at the mercy of the landlord and without the protection of the law, can not have a very stimulating effect upon Jewish agriculture.

INDEPENDENT FARMING.

Besides Jewish labor, Jewish capital also has been applied to agricultural enterprises. Before the emancipation of the peasants there could have been no inducement for Jewish capital to enter the field of landowning, because the possession of serfs was the exclusive privilege of the nobility, and outside of the serfs there existed no supply of labor to enable the proprietor to cultivate his land. No sooner had the emancipation of the serfs been realized than the Polish insurrection caused the prohibition, in 1863, of land purchases by Jews within nine Provinces of the west. Finally, the laws of 1882 practically stopped further purchases and greatly reduced the cases of renting of land to Jews, since such tenancy, being unrecognized by law, became a very risky enterprise for the Jewish tenant.

Nevertheless, considerable tracts of land are still owned or rented by Jews. The central statistical committee, the main official statistical office of the Russian Government, recently stated the area of land in Jewish hands to be as follows:

	Acres.
Fifteen Provinces of the Pale	3, 409, 916
Ten Polish Provinces	926, 913
Total in the Pale	4, 336, 829
All other European Russia	2, 014, 735
Caucasus	13, 705
Siberia	50, 671
Middle Asia	6, 744
Total in the Empire	6, 422, 684

Although this area is considerable, it is only a small part of the total area of the country. In the Pale, where Jewish occupancy of estates is most common, it does not exceed 1.5 per cent; and only in Poland, where the restrictions of Jewish land occupation are least stringent, does the proportion reach 2.5 per cent of the land area or more than 5 per cent of the land in private ownership, that is, the land not in the possession of the peasants. In Poland, of the land occupied by the Jews, 86 per cent is owned and 14 per cent is leased; in the remaining Provinces of the Pale 32.5 per cent is owned and 67.5

per cent is leased.   The difference is evidently to be explained by the differences of the legal conditions in the two regions, caused by the May laws of 1882.   Some twenty years ago the central statistical committee published the results of a similar investigation for twelve Provinces of the Pale.   It is thus possible to make a comparison between Jewish land occupancy in 1881 (before the May laws) and in 1900, for these twelve Provinces of the Pale.   The Provinces of Vilna, Minsk, Moheelev, and the ten Provinces of Poland are not included.

JEWISH LANDHOLDINGS IN TWELVE PROVINCES OF THE PALE, 1900 COMPARED WITH 1881, BY TENURE.

Tenure of farms.	Acres in 1881.	Acres in 1900.	Decrease.	
			Acres.	Per cent.
Owned	1,847,879	1,022,418	825,461	44.7
Rented	5,400,374	785,523	4,614,851	85.5
Total	7,248,253	1,807,941	5,440,312	75.1

The Jewish Colonization Society made an independent investigation of these estates, which included 1,210,796 dessiatines (3,271,571 acres), or practically the entire area owned by Jews.   The investigation showed that practically all of the land is in the hands of owners of large estates, and only a small part (less than 1.5 per cent) belonged to those persons owning a farm so small that the proprietor probably gave to it his labor as well as his capital and management.

The following table shows the number and area of farms owned by Jews in twelve Provinces of the Pale, by size of farms:

NUMBER AND AREA OF FARMS OWNED BY JEWS IN TWELVE PROVINCES OF THE PALE, BY SIZE OF FARMS, 1898.

Size of farms.	Farms.		Area (acres).	Per cent of area.	Average size of farm (acres).
	Number.	Per cent.			
Under 54 acres	2,058	45.5	46,796	1.4	23
54 to 270 acres	821	18.2	118,183	3.6	144
Over 270 acres	1,642	36.3	3,106,592	95.0	1,892
Total	4,521	100.0	3,271,571	100.0	724

The question of the fitness of the Russian Jew for agricultural pursuits has often been discussed in connection with the problem of immigration and the congestion of Jewish immigrants in a few large cities of the United States, and the importance of distributing the Jewish as well as the other immigrants over the rural districts and of encouraging them to engage in agricultural pursuits has been emphasized.

It can scarcely be expected that agriculture will absorb a large part of the inflowing stream of Russian Jewish immigration, but the fact should not be overlooked that, notwithstanding many difficulties, thousands of Jews have gone into agriculture in the United States, and the movement has shown a healthy growth, partly because the wave of emigration, which until recently was limited to Lithuania and White Russia, has extended into southwestern and southern Russia, and partly because of the much better organization of assistance to the intending Jewish farmer. Many efforts to organize Jewish agricultural grain-raising colonies have been complete failures. It has since been discovered by persons and institutions interested in Jewish colonization that special forms of farming offer a much better chance of success. The reports of the Jewish Agricultural and Industrial Aid Society indicate that while the few scattered farmers in the western and the northwestern sections of the United States are struggling for a precarious existence, many hundreds of Jewish farmers have established themselves quite successfully upon the "abandoned farms" of New England and by means of truck and dairy farming in the vicinity of large towns are generally laying the foundation of comfortable homes.

Within the last three years this society h‸s come in contact with over 1,000 Jewish farmers, most of whom were Russian Jews, and the following data relating to these farmers were collected by the society:

NUMBER OF FAMILIES, PERSONS, AND ACRES OF LAND AND VALUE OF REAL ESTATE AND PERSONAL PROPERTY OF JEWISH FARMERS IN AMERICA, BY LOCALITIES.

Locality.	Number of families.	Number of persons.	Land (acres).	Value of real estate.	Value of personal property.
Northern New Jersey	69	417	3,657	$171,170	$30,715
Southern New Jersey	242	1,358	6,190	291,115	49,585
New England	334	1,963	31,388	517,020	121,140
New York	161	832	14,029	368,105	70,310
Central and Middle West	46	328	3,878	80,100	21,015
Northwestern States and Northwest Territory of Canada	243	1,298	46,605	267,450	156,960
Total	1,095	6,196	105,747	1,694,960	449,725

ARTISANS.

NUMBER OF WORKERS.

The natural difficulties of a removal of an urban people to the rural districts, in conjunction with the legal conditions, have been sufficient to keep the majority of the Jewish population of Russia in other than agricultural pursuits. This is clearly indicated by the occupation statistics of the census of 1897, quoted in a preceding section of this article.

But these figures must be read in the light of Russian economic conditions. When measured by the American standard the factory system in Russia is still in its infancy, and of the many thousands of Jews engaged in manufacturing and mechanical pursuits (to use the familiar phrase of the United States census) the great majority are artisans or handicraftsmen.

Since the Russian census of 1897 does not draw this line, the material gathered by the Jewish Colonization Society remains the best and most up-to-date source of information—at least as far as the statistical study of this problem is concerned.

The agents and correspondents of this society registered 500,986 artisans, and, since the total number of Jews gainfully employed was found to be a little over 1,500,000, the artisans constituted at least one-third.   As a matter of fact, however, it was practically impossible for a private statistical investigation to cover the entire Pale, and many artisans undoubtedly were omitted.   It is stated that the 500,986 artisans constituted 13.2 per cent of the Jewish population of the localities investigated, and as persons gainfully employed equaled 30 per cent of the Jewish population it follows that the artisans included 44 per cent of the entire Jewish working population. It is not necessary to lay too much emphasis upon this high percentage, which considerably exceeds the percentage of all industrial workers as obtained from the census, because the deduction that a very great proportion of the Jews earn their livelihood by manual labor is beyond dispute.   Undoubtedly this is a higher proportion of artisans than any other country shows.   The Jewish artisans, however, supply the demand for industrial products not only of the Jewish population, but of the entire population of the Pale.

Nevertheless, the extreme poverty of the Jewish artisans, which will be illustrated by statistical data, and the large proportion of skilled laborers or artisans among the immigrants to this country betray the overcrowded condition of the trades within the Russian Pale.   The condition of the clothing trade may be taken as an illustration.   Very little factory-made clothing is used in Russia, and practically all the tailors in that country come under the class of artisans, which class, it is necessary to point out, has a legal entity in Russia.   The census figures show that in a population of 42,338,567 within the Pale, 458,545 persons are occupied in the clothing trade, or 109 to each 10,000, while in the rest of the Russian Empire there were 700,320 persons in the trade in a population of 83,301,454, or only 84 per 10,000.

The overcrowding of the Pale with artisans, the insufficient number of such workmen in the rest of Russia, the extreme poverty of the Jewish artisans caused by this overcrowding of the market, and, finally, the usefulness of the Jewish artisans and the desirability of their distribution influenced the Russian Government to raise the barriers of the Pale for some artisans.   Throughout the first half of the nineteenth century these were principally distillers of spirits, but in 1865 the right to live outside the Pale was extended to all Jewish artisans. The report of the minister of internal affairs accompanying the law of June 28 (July 10), 1865, states that according to the reports of the governors of the Provinces of the Pale the extreme poverty of the artisans within the Pale is a result of the enforced overcrowding of that region with artisans; that the overcrowding is caused by the legal limitations of the Jew's right of domicile, and that not only the Jewish but non-Jewish artisans of the Pale suffer from this enforced overcrowding. The Jewish artisans, the minister said, are forced to cut the prices for orders, and the resulting competition affects all the artisans unfavorably. And yet the Jewish artisans were the most useful element among the Jews, and if it was found possible to grant the Jewish merchants the right to live in the interior of Russia, the artisans, it was argued, surely were worthy of the same privilege.

The law of 1865 was the result of these arguments. The natural question will be asked why the Jewish artisans have not overrun Russia, instead of flocking in such numbers to foreign lands, like the United States or the United Kingdom. The prospect of better earnings in foreign lands may serve as a partial explanation; but no less important is the extreme complexity of the law, and the subsequent amendments to it, which makes the legal position of a Jewish artisan in the interior of Russia very insecure. Thus a well-known text-book of special legislation relating to Jews devotes forty pages to commentaries and decisions regarding the right of the Jewish artisans to live beyond the limits of the Pale. The Jewish artisan is obliged to obtain from the artisans' guild a certificate of proficiency in the trade chosen, which certificate is granted only after an examination; he is obliged to have a certificate from the local authorities, as to his record; in his new place of residence he is strictly bound to his special trade, and not only is he obliged to be actively engaged in his trade, but he is also strictly prohibited from working at anything outside of it. The closest supervision over the fulfillment of these requirements is kept up by the police, and the artisan is liable to summary expulsion from his new place of residence for any infringement of these regulations. He is not permitted to deal in any products not made in his shop; so that a watchmaker, for instance, can not sell any watches unless put together by him, and under no circumstances can he sell a watch chain or fob. Many artisans are forced to return to the Pale when too old to work at their trade, and the children when they reach maturity are required to leave for the Pale unless they have qualified for a trade. The total number of Jewish artisan shops in fifteen of the most important Provinces of the interior of Russia, according to an official investigation in 1893, was ascertained to be less than 2,000, and the total number of Jewish artisans outside the Pale was estimated at considerably less than 10,000.

The distribution of the artisans through the four main divisions of the Pale, as well as the distribution according to the main classes of occupations, are shown in the following table compiled from the report of the Jewish Colonization Society:

NUMBER AND PER CENT OF JEWISH ARTISANS IN EACH CLASSIFIED OCCUPATION IN THE FOUR MAIN DIVISIONS OF THE PALE, 1898.

Class of occupation.	Northwestern Russia.	Southwestern Russia.	Southern (new) Russia.	Poland.	Total.	Per cent.
Clothing and wearing apparel	60,637	56,240	26,228	50,854	193,954	38.7
Leather goods	32,292	21,853	9,348	21,813	85,306	17.0
Food products	23,174	14,401	5,083	15,229	57,887	11.6
Wood manufactures	19,791	16,382	5,276	8,139	49,588	9.9
Metals	16,667	15,706	8,553	7,995	48,921	9.8
Chemicals	1,535	1,198	322	562	3,617	.7
Building and ceramics	14,754	8,007	3,411	5,418	31,590	6.3
Textiles	6,993	3,422	809	7,204	18,428	3.7
Paper and stationery	3,660	3,640	2,238	2,157	11,695	2.3
Total	179,503	140,849	61,263	119,371	500,986	100.0
Per cent of artisans of Jewish population	12.6	9.9	8.4	9.0	10.2	....

When this table is compared with the table on page 491, giving the distribution of the Jewish population, the interesting fact is noticed that the larger the proportion of the Jewish population to the total population the larger is the proportion of artisans to the Jewish population. Thus, in northwestern Russia, where the Jews constitute 14.1 per cent of the total population, the proportion of artisans among the Jews is 12.6 per cent; in Poland the proportions are 14.1 per cent and 9.0 per cent; in southwestern Russia, 9.7 per cent and 9.9 per cent; in southern (new) Russia, 9 per cent and 8.4 per cent. It is only in Poland that this regularity of decrease is slightly disturbed, which may be due to the fact that the legal rights of the Jews in Poland are less limited than in the rest of the Pale. As a rule, however, a large proportion of Jews are forced into trades, because of the difficulty of earning a living in other walks of life, while their dispersion among other nationalities, especially those of a lower culture, stimulates them to adopt a commercial career. The same difference may be noticed in the United States, when the occupations of the Jews in New York City are compared with the occupations of Jews in the southern cities.

The classification of the artisans into nine main groups shows that the great majority of the Jewish artisans supply the immediate wants of the neighborhood, producing goods mainly for immediate consumption; thus, 38.7 per cent are occupied in the production of clothing and other wearing apparel and 17.0 per cent in the manufacture of leather goods, i. e., boots and shoes, gloves, and harness. Likewise the workers in the groups of food products, of wood manufactures, and even that of metal manufactures, produce for the immediate demands of the neighborhood, as do most of the artisans belonging to the group of building trades and the ceramic industry.

On the other hand, the last three or four groups include many trades in which a wider market for the products is necessary, and in these the artisan's trade loses the character of a neighborhood industry. In the class of chemical industry are included such trades as the makers of ink, shoe blacking, dyes, soap, candles, turpentine, and tar; the ceramic industry includes brick and tile makers; the textiles group consists of weavers, rope makers, and brush makers; the last group embraces the printing trades and the stationery trades.

Most of the trades enumerated do not manufacture to order only— do not employ the customer's material—and the artisan approaches more nearly the domestic industry, or even the small factory.

It is unfortunately impossible to determine from the data in hand what proportion of the 500,000 registered artisans are working for wages. The authors in the report from which most of the data have been obtained venture to take the proportion between master workmen, journeymen, and apprentices as a measure of the size of an average artisan's shop, evidently on the supposition that the former are usually independent artisans. But their own data frequently furnish convincing refutation of this hypothesis. For instance, in the case of the manufacture of agricultural machinery in the small town of Rakov we find 8 artisans' shops, which employ 23 master workmen, 37 journeymen, and 15 apprentices, or 75 persons, of whom only 8 are the proprietors. Nevertheless, the number of the journeymen is at least indicative of the number of wageworkers. Of the 500,986 artisans, 259,396 were masters, 140,528 were journeymen, and 101,062 were apprentices. The minimum number of wageworkers was, therefore, at least 241,590, or 48.2 per cent; in reality it was much greater. Besides the masters, who are forced to work for other masters, there must certainly be counted as wageworkers those persons who work for a middleman and use his material, as is shown to be the case with the knit-goods makers of Vilna.

WOMEN AND CHILDREN IN THE HAND TRADES.

The proverbial sanctity of the Jewish home has for many generations kept the Jewish woman out of industrial life. While it was not unusual for a Jewish woman of the middle class to continue the business after the death of her husband, or under other exceptional circumstances, the appearance of the Jewish girl or woman in the factory or even in the artisan's shop is comparatively recent. Of the

500,000 artisans, there were 76,548 women and girls, who were distributed as follows:

JEWISH FEMALE ARTISANS COMPARED WITH TOTAL JEWISH ARTISANS, BY
REGIONS, 1898.

Region.	Total artisans.	Female artisans.	
		Number.	Per cent of total artisans.
Northwestern Russia	179,503	31,800	17.7
Southwestern Russia	140,849	21,233	15.1
Southern (new) Russia	61,263	8,581	14.0
Poland	119,371	14,934	12.5
Total	500,986	76,548	15.3

The difference in the percentages which women constitute of the entire class of artisans in various sections of the Pale is significant, in view of the greater poverty and greater overcrowding of the Jews in the northwestern Provinces.

The limitations of a private investigation did not permit a detailed inquiry into the ages of the workers, but the organization of the artisan guild indirectly furnishes information in regard to the extension of child labor. The Russian artisan guild, like the mediæval prototype, recognizes three grades—the master workman, the journeyman, and the apprentice, the latter being invariably a minor and usually under 14 years of age at the beginning of apprenticeship. Thus the number of apprentices gives the number of children employed.

Altogether there were 101,062 apprentices, of whom 79,169 were boys and 21,893 were girls. For the entire Pale the proportion was as follows: Men, 68.9 per cent; women, 10.9 per cent; boys, 15.8 per cent; girls, 4.4 per cent. The number and per cent of men, women, boys, and girls employed in the trades in the four different regions of the Pale are shown in the following table:

NUMBER AND PER CENT OF JEWISH MEN, WOMEN, BOYS, AND GIRLS ENGAGED IN
THE TRADES IN EACH REGION OF THE PALE, 1898.

Class.	Northwestern Russia.		Southwestern Russia.		Southern (new) Russia.		Poland.		Total in Pale.	
	Number.	Per cent.	Number.	Per cent.	Number.	Per cent.	Number.	Per cent.	Number.	Per cent.
Men	119,481	66.6	99,858	70.9	42,310	69.1	83,620	70.1	345,269	68.9
Women	21,990	12.2	16,120	11.5	6,010	9.8	10,535	8.8	54,655	10.9
Boys	28,222	15.7	19,758	14.0	10,372	16.9	20,817	17.4	79,169	15.8
Girls	9,810	5.5	5,113	3.6	2,571	4.2	4,399	3.7	21,893	4.4
Total	179,503	100.0	140,849	100.0	61,263	100.0	119,371	100.0	500,986	100.0

Here also northwestern Russia makes the poorest showing, having the largest proportion of women and girls, and the number of men falls to two-thirds of the entire number of artisans.

As one might expect, the greater number of the females are found in a limited number of trades. Thus, 49,950 of them are employed as dressmakers and seamstresses (two-thirds of the total number employed), 4,014 are milliners, 5,700 are knit-goods makers, and 1,700 are cigarette makers. These trades comprise over 80 per cent of the total number of females employed.

MARKETING OF THE PRODUCTS.

Although the enumeration of the various trades is in itself sufficient to show that the typical method of the mediæval artisan of producing to the order of the individual consumer is not the only method used by the Jewish artisans, a study of the various methods of marketing these products confirms the induction that the artisan is developing into a petty manufacturer. The prohibition of living in the village forces the Jewish artisan—the tailor or the shoemaker—to seek his natural and most important customer, the peasant, in a more indirect way. This he does by visiting the many fairs frequented by the peasant; but this method of conducting a business has the serious drawback that it consumes a great deal of the artisan's time. Because of this a class of middlemen has naturally grown up who give large orders. By means of these middlemen the range of the market has gradually extended, so that it is not unusual to find artisans who work for these intermediaries exclusively. The small city of Radom, in Poland, sends out annually shoes to the value of about 1,000,000 rubles ($515,000); in Vitebsk the tailors work mainly for the dealers in ready-made clothing, a trade condition that approaches the system of contracting which is so familiar to students of economic conditions in New York City; in Dubrovna, a small town of the Province of Moheelev, a large proportion of the population is specialized in weaving "taleisim," peculiar towel-like cloths used for religious purposes, and here about 500 artisans are completely dependent upon three or four middlemen, who buy the entire product of the industry and find a market for it throughout the Pale. Usually many members of the family work at the same trade, which combines all the objectionable features of the sweat-shop and the domestic-factory system. The causes of the growth of the system are the same in the Pale as those which have brought about the development of the domestic system, and later the factory, in many industrial countries; namely, the lack of capital, the impossibility of borrowing except at usurious rates of interest, and, in addition, the strong competition in many trades of factory-made goods. The poor "independent" artisan often has not the money to buy even the material for a small private order, to say nothing of buying the necessary machinery that has gradually forced its way into the hand trades.

A characteristic instance of this is found in the knitting industry in the city and Province of Vilna. From 1,000 to 2,000 women in the Province are employed in this industry. A very small proportion of them work in factories that are provided with steam power, because the majority of the manufacturers (for the middlemen in this instance are middlemen in name only) prefer not to have the expense of rent and supervision, especially since factory inspection and all labor legislation do not apply to the artisan shops and to domestic industry. These manufacturers, therefore, buy the knitting machines, place them in the homes of the workingwomen, supply the necessary yarn, and pay the women piecework wages. Surely, there is very little of the independent artisan left under such an arrangement of an industry.

With the growth of the market several cities are specializing in one line of trade or other. In the small Polish town of Bresin a large number of tailors work for dealers in ready-made clothing, who visit the town several times a year, coming from all over the south. Several towns of the Polish Province of Siedlec have specialized in brush making. In the Province of Grodno shoe and boot making is the principal occupation of a large part of the Jewish population. In several towns of the Province of Vitebsk the production of agricultural machinery has grown rapidly within the last few years. These artisans' shops, which employ a considerable number of hired laborers, differ little from factories.

CONDITIONS OF WORK.

The artisan's home is the artisan's shop. And while sentimentalists may consider it one of the advantages of the artisan's work, because of its tendency to preserve the home, in reality it is one of the greatest drawbacks in the life of the artisan's family. It is not the function of the home to be the workshop, and the combination is specially harmful where the homes are as small, crowded, and poverty-stricken as are the majority of Jewish homes within the Pale. The following is a fair description by a Russian writer of the condition of the Jewish artisans' homes in one of the largest towns of the Jewish Pale, the city of Moheelev, which has a population of about 50,000 and is the capital of the Province of the same name:

The homes of the artisans are small and crowded. But no matter how small and crowded, tenants are often admitted, and there is seldom more than one room for a family. The room serves as kitchen, living and sleeping room, and workshop. And it is not unusual for a tailor to rent the same room for school purposes, so that instruction is served to a small class of private pupils in the same room where the tailor works with his apprentice; the tailor's wife cooks the food and washes the clothes, and the tailor's prolific family mingles its joyful noise with the monotonous chanting of the Hebrew teacher and the scholars.[a]

---

[a] See Die Organizationen des Judischen Proletariats in Russland, von Sara Rabinowitsch. Karlsruhe, 1903.

It is impossible to expect any regulation of the working-day under conditions such as described above. The independent artisan who works on his own account is only too happy to have any work to do, and, unless idle for lack of orders, works as long as it is possible to work. Still worse is (or was until the very recent epidemic of strikes changed conditions considerably) the situation in the larger artisans' shops, which are virtually sweat shops of the worst order. The factory legislation is not applicable to such industrial establishments; the workingmen or workingwomen live, eat, and sleep in the workroom, and, being under constant supervision, the only limitation upon the working-day is the generosity of the proprietor of the shop. During the busy season the girls in the dressmaking establishments may work from 6 o'clock in the morning until 12 midnight. In Moheelev "the normal working-day of the seamstresses lasts 12 hours, while during the winters it may be prolonged to 14, 16, and even 18 hours."

The organization of the Jewish workingmen dates from the end of the last century, and the strikes that followed showed immediate improvement in the condition of the factory workers as well as of the artisans.

In Vitebsk the working-day of all the Jewish artisans, which had been from 13 to 18 hours, was in 1898 reduced to 10 to 12 hours. In Homel the reduction was as great, the 16 to 17 hour working-day of the tailors being reduced to 14 to 15 hours net; of the joiners from 17 hours to 13 to 14 hours net; of the locksmiths, from 16 hours to 14 hours net; of the shoemakers, from 18 hours to 15 hours net; of the dressmakers, from 16 hours to 13 to 14 hours net.

These long working hours have been, until recently, a feature of all Russian industry; and, as a rule, the hours of work in the artisans' shops which do not come under the provisions of the factory legislation are invariably longer. But in view of the great changes in the political as well as the economic life of Russia, which are taking place at present, it is difficult to say what the average working-day is. Undoubtedly many factories, and many more artisans' shops in the interior of the country, still keep up a very long day of 13 to 15 hours; yet the workday of 10 and even 9 hours has been introduced in many establishments in St. Petersburg and in Moscow. There is no information of such shortening of the labor day in the industrial centers of the Pale, but even in that section the actual working-day varies greatly.

The following illustrations of successful reductions of the hours of labor, for the years 1903 and 1904, by means of strikes have been gleaned from the Letzte Nachrichten, the official organ of the "Universal Union of the Jewish Workingmen in Lithuania, Poland, and

Russia," and published until recently in Switzerland. During the last two or three years the extraordinary political activity of this organization has forced it to neglect its economic activity.

In Lodz, the Manchester of Russian Poland, the bakers, in the summer of 1903, struck for the reduction of the hours of labor from 15 to 13 and were successful.[a]   In the small town of Prilooki, in the Province of Poltava, the workingmen of the local tobacco factory succeeded, in August, 1903, in having the hours of labor reduced from 13 to 10½.[b]   During the same month the locksmiths of Vitebsk, the capital city of the province of the same name, had their hours reduced from 13 to 12.[c]   In Radomysl, Province of Kiev, the tailors, as a result of a strike which lasted one day and a half, had the working-day of from 17 to 18 hours reduced to 14 hours.[d]

These few quoted instances show that the Jewish workingmen, even in the small establishments of the artisans, are fully alive to the gravity of an abnormally long working-day and are persistently striving to shorten it.

WAGES AND EARNINGS.

In the absence of systematic wage statistics in Russia it is futile to try to determine the average wages of the artisans' employees. Still more difficult is it to speak with any degree of accuracy of the average earnings of the army of small independent artisans, since these earnings must of necessity be subject to great variations, both of place and time and from one artisan to another. Nevertheless, the usual estimates furnished by local correspondents well acquainted with local conditions are of some value. From some reports a number of such estimates were gathered, and these estimates are presented in the following tabular statement:

EARNINGS OF JEWISH ARTISANS, BY LOCALITIES AND BY OCCUPATIONS, 1898.

Locality.	Occupation.	Earnings per annum.
Lithuania:		
Vilna (town of Vilna)	Knit-goods operatives (women)	e $1.29 to $1.80
Vilna (town of Vilna)	Knit-goods operatives (men)	38.63 to 51.50
Vilna (town of Vilna)	Knit-goods operatives(men, high)	128.75 to 154.50
Kovno (town of Kovno)	Shoemakers (high)	206.00 to 257.50
Grodno (town of Grodno)	Shoemakers	154.50 to 206.00
Grodno (town of Grodno)	Shoemakers (average)	77.25 to 103.00
Grodno (town of Grodno)	Tailors	77.25 to 257.50
White Russia:		
Minsk (town of Minsk)	Knit-goods operatives (women)	38.63 to 51.50
Minsk (town of Slootsk)	Shoemakers	e 1.55 to 3.09
Vitebsk (town of Vitebsk)	Blacksmiths	e 2.58 to 3.09
Vitebsk (town of Vitebsk)	Carpenters	e 2.06 to 2.58
Vitebsk (town of Vitebsk)	Potters	185.40
Southwestern Russia:		
Volhynia (35 localities)	Tailors	61.80 to 103.00
Volhynia (26 localities)	Tailors	103.00 to 154.50
Kiev (17 localities)	Tailors	77.25 to 103.00

a Letze Nachrichten, No. 139.   d Letze Nachrichten, No. 185.
b Letze Nachrichten, No. 144.   e Per week.
c Letze Nachrichten, No. 146.

EARNINGS OF JEWISH ARTISANS, BY LOCALITIES AND BY OCCUPATIONS, 1898—Concluded.

Locality.	Occupation.	Earnings per annum.
Southwestern Russia—Concluded.		
Kiev (34 localities)	Tailors	$115.88 to 154.50
Kiev (9 localities)	Tailors	180.25 to 206.00
Kiev (7 localities)	Tailors	257.50 to 309.00
Podolia (42 localities)	Tailors	51.50 to 103.00
Podolia (32 localities)	Tailors	103.00 to 154.50
Poltava (17 localities)	Tailors	92.70 to 154.50
Poltava (5 localities)	Tailors	180.25 to 257.50
Volhynia (12 localities)	Shoemakers	51.50
Volhynia (12 localities)	Shoemakers	51.50 to 77.25
Volhynia (13 localities)	Shoemakers	77.25 to 103.00
Volhynia (25 localities)	Shoemakers	103.00 to 154.50
Kiev (24 localities)	Shoemakers	77.25 to 103.00
Kiev (31 localities)	Shoemakers	103.00 to 154.50
Kiev (8 localities)	Shoemakers	180.25 to 257.50
Podolia (16 localities)	Shoemakers	77.25
Podolia (21 localities)	Shoemakers	77.25 to 103.00
Podolia (24 localities)	Shoemakers	118.45 to 154.50
Kiev (31 localities)	Carpenters	103.00 to 154.50
Kiev (9 localities)	Carpenters	128.75 to 257.50
Volhynia (35 localities)	Carpenters	77.25 to 103.00
Volhynia (12 localities)	Carpenters	115.88 to 154.50
Volhynia (7 localities)	Carpenters	38.63 to 90.13
Podolia (16 localities)	Carpenters	51.50 to 77.25
Podolia (22 localities)	Carpenters	84.98 to 103.00
Podolia (20 localities)	Carpenters	128.75 to 154.50
Volhynia (13 localities)	Seamstresses	12.88 to 25.75
Volhynia (20 localities)	Seamstresses	25.75 to 51.50
Volhynia (13 localities)	Seamstresses	61.80 to 103.00
Kiev (33 localities)	Seamstresses	25.75 to 51.50
Kiev (18 localities)	Seamstresses	61.80 to 103.00
Podolia (52 localities)	Seamstresses	15.45 to 51.50
Podolia (16 localities)	Seamstresses	64.38 to 103.00
Poland:		
Thirty-three per cent of the localities	Tailors and dressmakers	Under 128.75
Forty-seven per cent of the localities	Tailors and dressmakers	128.75 to 154.50
Twenty per cent of the localities	Tailors and dressmakers	154.50 or over
Fifty-two per cent of the localities	Shoemakers	Under 128.75
Thirty-three per cent of the localities	Shoemakers	128.75 to 154.50
Fifteen per cent of the localities	Shoemakers	154.50 or over.
Town of Lodz	Brush makers	103.00 to 206.00
Town of Lodz	Weavers (at home)	a 3.09 to 3.61
Small towns	Lace makers (girls)	23.18 or over.
South Russia:		
Fifty-four localities	Tailors	128.75 to 206.00
Fourteen localities	Tailors	206.00 or over.
Fifty-five per cent of all localities	Seamstresses	51.50 to 206.00
Forty-five per cent of all localities	Seamstresses	Under 51.50

a Per week.

These money earnings must not be judged from the standpoint of American prices and the purchasing value of the dollar in the United States, for while the ruble is the equivalent of only 51.5 cents, yet its purchasing value in the majority of the cities of the Pale, with the exception of large cities like Odessa and Warsaw, is about equal to that of the American dollar. Even with this qualification, the earnings of the majority of the artisans are very small, and in view of the determination of the normal Jewish family's budget in a small town as 300 rubles ($154.50), a vast number of these artisans seem to have considerable difficulty in earning the necessary minimum.

The following table, compiled by the Jewish Colonization Society in its report on the economic condition of the Jews in Russia, gives the earnings of a number of Jewish artisans in the cities of southern Russia:

JEWISH ARTISANS REPORTED IN THE CITIES OF SOUTHERN RUSSIA RECEIVING EACH CLASSIFIED AMOUNT OF ANNUAL EARNINGS, 1898.

Annual earnings.	Number of artisans reported in cities having a population of—			Total artisans reported.	
	Under 10,000.	10,000 to 50,000.	50,000 or over.	Number.	Per cent.
$51.50 or under	57	44		101	6.9
$52.02 to $128.75	379	199	32	610	41.6
$129.27 to $206.00	176	217	74	467	31.9
$206.52 to $283.25	57	62	32	151	10.3
$283.77 to $360.50	12	50	25	87	6.0
$361.02 to $437.75		10	11	21	1.4
$438.27 to $515.00		5	13	18	1.2
$515.52 or over		7	3	10	.7

The earnings of the artisans in the southern cities are evidently much higher than in the northwest, and in the larger cities reach a level practically unknown in Lithuania or in White Russia. These data are a sufficient explanation of the movement of the Jews southward, as well as of the absence of any perceptible Jewish emigration from the southern Provinces until it was stimulated by other than normal economic causes, namely the anti-Jewish riots.

ORGANIZATIONS OF ARTISANS.

The tendency toward improving the condition of work of the journeymen has been illustrated above. Some information of the Jewish labor movement of the last few years has reached the American press. This broad labor movement under the auspices of the powerful "Universal Union of Jewish Workingmen in Lithuania, Poland, and Russia" (the so-called "Bund"), which primarily directs its efforts toward the organization of the factory workers, will be discussed fully in another section of this article. Very little is known outside of the Pale of a peculiarly Jewish organization among the artisans and their employees, which antedated the "Bund" by many decades and must have prepared the way for the broader movement which was to follow. This organization is the so-called "khevra," a word of Hebrew origin, meaning a company, an association.

To a certain extent the "khevra" as it exists to-day is analogous to the artisans' guilds and journeymen's guilds of the Middle Ages in western Europe. Its origin, however, must be sought in the rites of the Jewish religion. Various Hebrew religious functions must be observed in common. In fact, the prayers on certain occasions must be held in the .presence of at least ten adults of the Jewish faith. Again, the main accessory of the Hebrew devotional exercises—the "thora" (the Old Testament, written in Hebrew on a long roll of parchment)—is too expensive to be in the possession of any but the richest citizens of the community. Thus, organizations for the express purpose of praying and of owning a "thora" sprung up; and it was easy for these organizations to develop along trade lines, because of the natural leaning of people of the same occupations toward each other. Gradually charitable functions were added to the religious ones; but in the beginning even the charitable acts had a religious basis, such as the execution of the various ceremonies connected with the burying of the dead members of the "khevra." The members of the "khevra" must not only accompany the body of the dead to its last resting place but must also assemble daily during the entire month to say the customary prayers. More important from the social-economic point of view is the obligation to stay, in regular turn, with a sick "brother" throughout the night if necessary.

The transition from this service to a sick benefit fund is natural. To make such financial assistance possible, a small entrance fee and still smaller dues are provided, the first being often as small as 1 ruble (51.5 cents) and the latter only 4 or 5 copecks (2 or 2½ cents) or less per week. If this moderate income still leaves a surplus it may be used in granting the members small loans without any interest. This tendency toward mutual assistance leads to a strong bond among the members of the "khevra" and teaches them the advantages of cooperative activity along broader lines. This depends upon the constituency of the organization. The original "khevra" consisted exclusively or primarily of independent master workmen. This is still true of "khevras" in those industries where the average shop is small and the majority of the artisans employ few or no wageworkers. The few journeymen join the organization and do not of themselves represent any considerable force in it; but as the number of working-men grows, a feeling of dissatisfaction with the management of the "khevra" arises. In the original "khevra" the democratic spirit is manifested by trusting the election of the officers to lot, and thus in a mixed "khevra," i. e., one where both masters and employees are found among the members, the offices may be exclusively given to the employers, which causes the formation of distinct parties in the "khevra." One solution of the difficulty is the breaking up of the "khevra" into two branches—one composed of the employers and the other of the employees. Or again, where the number of the employees is proportionately large and the employers approach the small capitalist, the latter may lose all interest in the "khevra" and it becomes a purely labor organization.[a]

[a] Die Organizationen des Judischen Proletariats in Russland, von Sara Rabino-witsch. Karlsruhe, 1903.

Such development has been noticed in the city of Moheelev, the only town where the "khevras" have been carefully studied. In that city were found single "khevras" of independent artisans in the following trades: Shoemakers (from 50 to 60 members); jewelers and watchmakers; and tin, roof, and lock smiths (about 30 members). Double "khevras," i. e., separate organizations of the masters and the employees, were found in the trades of the ladies' tailors, carpenters, dyers, and stove builders. The "khevra" of the ladies' tailors' employees is one of the oldest and strongest. It included over 70 workingmen and was able not only to conduct a comparatively extensive benevolent activity, but also to influence, to some extent, the condition of labor. Thus, it has put an end to a customary irregularity of payment of wages, has forced wages upward, and has even carried through the principle of the closed shop, in fact if not in name, since only the members of this "khevra" are entitled to employment by the tailors. This "khevra" is open to all workmen above the age of 18 years, but the entrance fee is 10 rubles ($5.15).

These social tendencies manifest themselves eloquently among the mass of the Jewish workingmen even in this country. The large number of Jewish "khevras," lodges, clubs, fraternities, brotherhoods, and other organizations—frequently under American names and with the introduction of various rites—that are pursuing partly religious and partly charitable purposes, and often possessing national organizations, are in reality only an outgrowth of the primitive "khevras." It was in this habit of organization that the labor-union propaganda found such fertile soil among the mass of the Jewish workingmen in New York City.

UNSKILLED LABORERS.

It has been observed that the Russian Jewish immigrant in the United States takes very unwillingly to unskilled labor. Thus in New York City of the total foreign population (foreign born and native born of foreign parentage) 10 per cent are common laborers, while of the Russians only 2.4 per cent are so reported. Similarly in Russia the Jew who finds it impossible to earn a living in commerce chooses some skilled trade. Aside from the low social position of the unskilled laborer, the reasons for this disinclination to enter that field of work are to be found in the inferior physique of the underfed city-bred Jew. The Jew in southern Russia more frequently lives in the country, is generally of a much more powerful physique, and takes more readily to unskilled or (according to the Russian terminology) "black" labor. Another reason is found in the unlimited supply of unskilled labor furnished by the Russian peasant, especially in northwestern Russia. In the Provinces of southern (new) Russia, which are more sparsely settled and often suffer from scarcity of labor, the wages of agricultural labor are higher and the Jew, both of the city and the country, is more often drawn to it. The data in regard to unskilled Jewish labor are not very satisfactory. No data at all could be obtained in regard to the five large cities of Lodz, Odessa, Kiev, Kovno, and Moheelev. Outside of these five cities the number of unskilled laborers was 97,900, so that the total number was certainly considerably over 100,000. In this number are included many kinds of work which in this country are not classified with unskilled labor, as is shown in the following table:

NUMBER OF JEWISH UNSKILLED LABORERS IN THE FOUR PRINCIPAL DIVISIONS OF THE PALE (NOT INCLUDING THE CITIES OF LODZ, ODESSA, KIEV, KOVNO, AND MOHEELEV), BY OCCUPATIONS, 1898.

Occupation.	Poland.	North-western Russia.	South-western Russia.	Southern (new) Russia.	Total.
Agricultural laborers	882	3,814	5,824	2,381	12,901
Cabmen	2,884	4,981	3,520	1,875	13,260
Diggers and stonebreakers	681	1,379	550	376	2,986
Longshoremen and carriers	7,670	7,349	8,044	9,465	32,528
Lumbermen	411	2,263	590	1,022	4,286
Raftsmen	161	1,975	141	836	3,113
Ragpickers	1,155	1,988	1,034	124	4,301
Teamsters	3,327	5,916	2,919	6,657	18,819
Water carriers	1,404	1,054	1,844	1,076	5,378
Not specified	31	111	132	54	328
Total	18,606	30,830	24,598	23,866	97,900

Altogether, these occupations employ about 2 per cent of the total Jewish population (equivalent to about 7 per cent of the Jews gainfully employed). For reasons indicated above, the percentage rises to 3.3 per cent in southern Russia (or about 10 per cent of those employed) and falls to 1.4 per cent in Poland (4.2 per cent of those employed). This high proportion is due to the inclusion among the unskilled workers of workmen in trades of a more or less skilled nature, such as lumbermen, teamsters, and agricultural laborers.

The data of the preceding table are mainly interesting as showing that the hardest forms of physical labor are not unfamiliar to the Russian Jews. While some of the occupations are not familiar in this country, such as a water carrier or a ragpicker, comparatively few Jews remain in the other employments above enumerated when they migrate to this country or to England, because they come in competition with workers of other nationalities who are more fit for heavy work in the open air. It is probable that under the influence of economic distress the number of the Jews in these occupations in Russia is increasing, since the turning of city-bred men and women to hired agricultural labor is a very unusual economic phenomenon. It is also probable that the number of Jewish agricultural laborers would have been considerably greater had it not been for the laws of 1882, which preclude the possibility of the Jew wandering very far in quest of such labor, because he has no right to live in the rural districts.

The average daily wage of an agricultural laborer varies considerably from locality to locality and from one season to the other, being highest in the Provinces of southern Russia, where it varies from 50 copecks (25.8 cents) during sowing time to 1.50 rubles (77 cents) during harvest; and lowest in northwestern Russia, where the wages are 25 copecks and 50 copecks (12.9 and 25.8 cents). These wages are not supplemented with board, and if board is supplied, the wages are somewhat lower. The standard of living of an agricultural laborer in Russia may easily be judged from the fact that the cost of subsistence is officially estimated at from 45 to 50 rubles ($23.18 to $25.75) per annum, which equals about 6 cents per day. The regular daily ration of an agricultural laborer consists of about 4 pounds of bread, which is sometimes supplemented with a cucumber or a few onions. In the Provinces of southern Russia there is often a perceptible shortage of agricultural labor during harvest time. Nevertheless the same restrictions against the Jew furnishing his labor at this time remain in force, which causes the scale of wages to rise, for a short time at least, much above the given limits.

For obvious reasons the number of longshoremen and carriers shown in the table is greatest in southern Russia, and if the data for Odessa had been obtained the number would have been much greater, for many of the Jewish cities, especially Odessa and Nikolaiev, are important ports and conduct a great exporting trade in grain.

Speaking of these laborers a Russian investigator of the conditions in Odessa says: [a]

From their external appearance it is difficult to guess at their nationality, so strong, rough, and muscular do they look. Their wages, besides being very low, rarely more than 50 copecks [25.8 cents] for a whole day's work, are seldom regular, their employment almost accidental, and the large numbers of these laborers anxiously waiting for an opportunity to earn a few copecks, and crowding the so-called market (or the open public ground) is one of the most distressing pictures of each and every Russian-Jewish town.

The draymen's occupation was very popular among the Jews of the northwestern Provinces before the railroads were built, and in the smaller towns of the Pale, especially in the northwest and in Poland, it is still exclusively in the hands of the Jews. An official investigation of the 15 Provinces of the Pale (exclusive of the 10 Polish Provinces) made in 1887, determined the number of cabmen and teamsters at 18,532, and, according to the above table, the number had grown to 25,868 in 1898–99, and yet this increase of 39.6

---

[a] See V Cherte Evreiskoy Osedlosti (Within the Jewish Pale), by A. P. Subbotin. St. Petersburg, 1888. Vol. II, p. 228.

per cent within the short period of eleven years did not come because of exceptional prosperity in that occupation.   The development of the railway system in western Russia has curtailed the old form of transportation of passengers and to some extent of the freight among the towns of the Pale, which was a profitable business at one time. The rapid construction of electric tram lines in most of the larger cities of the Pale has had a similar effect upon the business of the city cabmen, who, before the advent of the electric lines, controlled the only mode of intraurban transportation.   There are still many towns in the Pale not connected by any railroad line, but most of them have lost their commercial importance, and the income of the old teamster, with his large, ugly, and dilapidated wagon, not unlike that used by the American pioneer in his migrations westward, has also fallen considerably.   In the large towns the new methods of transporting goods have developed; but in the development of the business the independence of the teamsters has been destroyed. Whether they get a stipulated wage, as do the cabmen in Warsaw, of board and 1 ruble (51.5 cents) a week, or are given a fixed percentage of their daily earnings, or get the residue after a certain minimum has been earned for their employer (as in Odessa), their incomes are invariably smaller than under the old system.   The average daily income of a teamster who does not possess his own team has been estimated at from 75 copecks to 1.5 rubles (38.6 to 77.3 cents), while the teamster or cabman who is the owner of his outfit may earn even from 2 to 2½ rubles ($1.03 to $1.29).

A very peculiar occupation, which is rapidly vanishing in the larger cities of the Pale, but which will probably remain for a long time in the middle-sized towns, is that of the water carrier.   Ten or twelve years ago even the larger cities of the Pale, such as the seats of the provincial governments, had no other provision for water supply than the river flowing by in the vicinity, and the distribution of water over the entire city was done in a very primitive manner.   Often the water carrier did not possess even a horse and wagon and a barrel. This primitive method is still in use in the smaller towns, where the poverty of the people precludes the possibility of constructing a system of waterworks.   A water carrier, even though he works incessantly, can not clear much more than 50 copecks (25.8 cents) a day.

Another specifically Russian occupation is that of the drivers of the sanitary wagons which, in most of the smaller Russian towns, serve as a substitute for a system of sewerage and drainage.   Probably because of the objectionable character of the work the daily income of the drivers of these wagons ranges from 80 copecks to 1½ rubles (41.2 to 77.3 cents).

MANUFACTURING INDUSTRY.

JEWISH BRANCHES OF INDUSTRY.

The emancipation of the serfs in 1863 gave to Russia an abundant supply of free labor, which naturally gravitated into the cities, and thus the industrial history of Russia since that time presents a growth of manufactures on a larger scale than was ever before known in that country. In western Russia the growth was most rapid, because the economic condition of the masses of Jews inhabiting the cities of the Pale was especially favorable to the growth of industries. Both Jewish commerce and Jewish hand trades had rapidly become less profitable; therefore Jewish capital and Jewish labor were attracted toward manufacturing. The following data for the two periods 1889 and 1897, separated only by the short period of nine years, illustrate the rapid growth of the industry in the Pale:

NUMBER OF MANUFACTURING PLANTS AND EMPLOYEES AND VALUE OF PRODUCTS, BY REGIONS, 1889 AND 1897.

[From official data published by the Russian ministry of finance.]

Region and year.	Mills and factories.	Employ- ees.	Value of products.
Northwestern Russia:			
1889	1,337	20,080	$11,466,475
1897	1,962	39,802	26,461,730
Southwestern Russia:			
1889	1,711	a 19,727	26,824,290
1897	2,596	42,613	38,599,250
Southern (new) Russia:			
1889	1,084	25,319	30,382,425
1897	2,562	99,170	119,228,165
The Pale (not including Poland):			
1889	4,132	a 65,126	68,673,190
1897	7,120	181,585	184,289,145
Per cent of increase	72.3	a 150.8	168.4

a Not including employees in the Province of Kiev. In 1897 the number of employees in that Province was 18,270, which number was deducted from the total in calculating the per cent of increase.

The greatest growth of industrial activity according to these official data is found in southern Russia, which is accounted for by the rich mineral deposits in that region. The northwestern Provinces are very poor in such deposits, and there the condition of the labor market was probably the greatest stimulus to the growth of the industry, and next to it were the efforts of Jewish enterprise. These considerations explain, for instance, why one of the greatest of the Russian tobacco factories grew up in a small and insignificant town like Grodno and why Bialystok, near Grodno, became a great textile center.

But this manufacturing industry is not all the result of Jewish enterprise. In fact, the proportion of Jewish capitalists is not so great as the number of Jews would lead one to expect.

In the first of the following tables, taken from the report of the St. Petersburg Jewish Colonization Society, is shown the number of factories in three regions of the Pale and the number and per cent of such factories operated by Jews; also the number of employees in all factories, the number and per cent of employees in Jewish factories, and the average number in each factory classed as non-Jewish and Jewish. The value of products manufactured by all the factories and the value and per cent of the products manufactured by Jewish factories are also given in the second table, as well as the average value by non-Jewish and by Jewish factories. A study of the figures reveals the fact that although in northwestern Russia the Jews controlled 51 per cent of all the factories and had 58.3 per cent of the total number of employees, the value of the products manufactured was only 47.6 per cent of the total. In the 15 Provinces the Jews had 37.8 per cent of the factories, employed only 27 per cent of the workingmen, and the value of products manufactured in Jewish factories was but 22.5 per cent of the total value of manufactured products. The averages, perhaps, indicate more clearly the smaller relative productiveness of Jewish factories as compared with non-Jewish factories. The tables show that while the average number of employees in each Jewish factory was considerably over one-half of the average number in each non-Jewish factory the average value of the manufactured products was less than one-half of that of the non-Jewish factory. This discrepancy is fully explained, however, by the fact that among the Jewish factories there is a larger percentage unprovided with any mechanical power.

NUMBER OF JEWISH FACTORIES AND EMPLOYEES COMPARED WITH TOTAL FACTORIES AND EMPLOYEES, IN THREE SPECIFIED REGIONS OF THE PALE, 1898.

[From Report of Jewish Colonization Society.]

Region.	Factories.			Employees.				
	Total.	Jewish.		Total.	In Jewish factories.		Average.	
		Number.	Per cent of total.		Number.	Per cent of total.	In non-Jewish factories.	In Jewish factories.
Northwestern Russia	2,749	1,402	51.0	51,659	30,105	58.3	16.0	21.5
Southwestern Russia	3,374	1,143	33.9	108,769	28,142	25.9	36.1	24.6
Southern (new) Russia	1,627	388	23.8	74,775	5,262	7.0	56.1	13.6
Total	7,750	2,933	37.8	235,203	63,509	27.0	35.6	21.7

VALUE OF PRODUCTS MANUFACTURED IN JEWISH FACTORIES COMPARED WITH
TOTAL VALUE OF MANUFACTURED PRODUCTS IN THREE SPECIFIED REGIONS OF
THE PALE, 1898.

[From Report of Jewish Colonization Society.]

Region.	Value of products manufactured.				
	Total.	In Jewish factories.		Average.	
		Total.	Per cent of total.	In non-Jewish factories.	In Jewish factories.
Northwestern Russia	$32,403,028	$15,430,894	47.6	$12,600	$11,006
Southwestern Russia	82,106,141	22,114,049	26.9	26,890	19,347
Southern (new) Russia	94,039,309	9,414,560	10.0	68,301	24,264
Total	208,548,478	46,959,503	22.5	33,546	16,011

Although in Russia there are no statistics of distribution of wealth
and no income statistics, it is still possible to draw the conclusion
that, notwithstanding the existence of a few wealthy Jewish manufacturers in northwestern Russia and in southern Russia, the average
Jewish manufacturer commands a much smaller capital than does
his non-Jewish competitor, and that the average Jewish factory is
in reality a very small establishment.

Besides the lack of Jewish capital there are undoubtedly other
factors, of a legal nature, which keep the Jews from establishing
large industrial enterprises.

One of the reasons why the participation of the Jews in this branch
of industry has been so insignificant is the fact that in the cities, where
purchase and renting of landed property is permitted to them, for
sanitary reasons not all kinds of factories and mills may be established, and the acquisition of real estate beyond the city limits was
prohibited by the laws of 1865; furthermore, the May laws of 1882
forbid them the renting of land and even settlement within the
villages.

The corporate form of organization is still little used in Russian
industry, especially in small establishments, and for a factory with
an average production valued at 20,000 to 40,000 rubles ($10,300 to
$20,600) per annum, the presence of the proprietor is an absolute
necessity. A small Jewish capitalist can not, therefore, establish a
factory in a locality in which he is denied the right of domicile.

In Russia Jewish capital has not that tendency to one-sidedness
which is so marked in the New World. Such capital may be found in
a great variety of industries, though some branches attract it more
than others. In the following list only those industries are mentioned in which Jewish capital and enterprise are more prominent
than in the others:

TOTAL FACTORIES, JEWISH FACTORIES, AND PER CENT OF JEWISH FACTORIES, BY INDUSTRIES.

Industry.	Total factories.	Jewish factories.	
		Number.	Per cent of total factories.
Textile	372	299	80.4
Lumber	329	199	60.5
Tobacco	110	83	75.5
Hides	530	287	54.2
Soap	139	122	87.8
Brick	752	157	20.9
Tiles	37	30	81.1
Flouring mill products	1,907	542	28.4
Creameries	159	80	50.3
Distilling	846	57	6.7
Beer brewing	381	110	28.9
Mineral waters	119	83	69.7

Smaller investments of Jewish capital may be found in dozens of other industries. Its participation in the beet-sugar industry is very great, that being one of the industries in which the corporate form of management has become customary, but the per cent of Jewish capital can not be determined. There are Jewish glass factories and iron and steel mills. More than one-half of the number of match factories and all the brush factories in the Pale belong to the Jews, and there are Jewish paper factories, machine shops, etc. Some twenty years ago the distillery business was almost altogether in the hands of Jews, but the difficulty of establishing themselves outside the limits of the cities has forced many of them out of this industry. The number of small Jewish beer breweries has also rapidly diminished because of the introduction of the Government monopoly in the sale of spirituous liquors. No less significant is the almost entire absence of Jewish capital from the mining and metallurgical industry, for reasons indicated above.

JEWISH INDUSTRIES IN POLAND.

The insufficiency of official data in regard to Polish industry leaves the data collected by the agents and correspondents of the Jewish Colonization Society the only source of information. During the last thirty years the industrial development of Poland has been very great, but German capitalists and business men much more than the Jewish were instrumental in fostering this development. A stream of German capital, energy, and experience has constantly flowed across the frontier, and a greater stream of labor has followed until Poland has become the great industrial center of the Russian Empire. Gradually domestic capital and enterprise and labor drifted into manufacturing industry, and this domestic capital meant Jewish capital. But Jewish factories still remain the weaker and smaller. Of the 4,221 factories officially registered in Poland, the correspondents of the Jewish Colonization Society reported on 1,867 only, of which number 1,416 belonged to Jewish and 451 to non-Jewish capitalists, but this must not be taken as a true proportion of the Jewish factories, because the correspondents devoted themselves especially to the description of the Jewish establishments. Nevertheless, it is significant to find that in a Jewish factory the average number of workingmen was 30, while in a non-Jewish factory it was 102. Moreover, of the Jewish factories only 27 per cent were provided with mechanical power, while of the non-Jewish factories 69 per cent had such power. If the factories be divided into two classes, those with and those without mechanical motors, it is found that of the factories with mechanical power, the non-Jewish had an average number of 135 workingmen and the Jewish only 72; of all the factories without mechanical power, the non-Jewish had an average number of 28 workingmen and the Jewish only 15 workingmen.

In the following statement is shown the number of establishments in the various branches of industry in which Jewish capital is employed:

Textiles	305	Lumber	46
Leather	162	Beer breweries	45
Creameries	98	Paper manufacture	42
Mineral waters	81	Chemical industry	29
Flour mills	68	Soap manufacture	28
Brick factories	66	Brushes, etc	25
Dry goods	63	All other	201
Manufactures of wood	58		
Glass and pottery	50	Total	1,416
Metal goods	49		

JEWISH ACTIVITY IN THE TEXTILE INDUSTRY.

The textile industry remains the most prominent industry of Poland, but recently several important centers of textile industry have sprung up in other regions of the Pale. Lodz, a city in the Polish Province of Petrikau, has within the comparatively short time of thirty or forty years become a great manufacturing center, and supplies cotton goods to the entire Russian Empire. Zgierz and Tomaszow, in the same Province, have developed into great centers of manufactures of woolen goods. In Lithuania the most important center of the textile industry is Bialystok, where woolen goods are manufactured. In Poland there are 305 Jewish factories of textile goods, of which number 155 are located in the city of Lodz. In the region of Bialystok (Province of Grodno) and its suburbs there are 299 Jewish factories out of a total of 372. Some of the greatest factories in Lodz belong to Jews, such as the cotton factories of Posnansky, Rosenblatt, Silberstein, and others. The first of these employs from 6,000 to 7,000 workingmen, and the value of its products is about 12,000,000 rubles ($6,180,000) each year. A few such establishments may distort any averages; nevertheless, it still remains true that the 155 Jewish textile factories employ 12,848 men, or about 83 workingmen per factory, while the 112 non-Jewish factories employ 31,593 men, or 282 workingmen per factory, and that of the Jewish factories 37 per cent have no mechanical power, while of the non-Jewish factories 14, or only 12.5 per cent, are without such power.

Even in Bialystok, which is much more of a Jewish manufacturing center than Lodz, the same inferiority of the Jewish factory is noticed. Thus of the 318 factories manufacturing woolen goods, 260 were Jewish and only 58 non-Jewish. The average value of the production of a Jewish factory was 16,800 rubles ($8,652) and the average number of workingmen 17; in a non-Jewish factory the average value of production was 73,000 rubles ($37,595), and the average number of workingmen was 55. In short, it must be admitted that notwithstanding a few individual cases, the number of great Jewish capitalists is small, and that the majority of the Jewish manufacturers are people of moderate means. It will appear presently that this circumstance has some important consequences upon the condition of Jewish labor.

FACTORY LABOR.

Jewish labor appeared in large manufacturing industries much later than Jewish capital and enterprise, and for obvious reasons. In the middle of the last century the majority of the Jews belonged to the middle class; they were either merchants or independent artisans and work in a factory presented to them a considerable downward step in the social scale. So it is natural to find that a strong prejudice existed against such action some thirty years ago, especially when the remuneration of a factory worker and the general conditions of his life and work were very unsatisfactory, as they always are in the initial stages of the development of capitalistic industry. It required a perceptible decline in the economic condition of the Jewish artisan, in the early eighties, to force him into the ranks of the industrial army. Since then the number of Jewish wageworkers in manufacturing industries has grown rapidly, but owing to the absence of official labor statistics it is impossible to state the number of these factory workers with any degree of accuracy. The only source for even approximate information upon this most important problem remains in the data collected by the agents of the Jewish Colonization Society for their report on the economic condition of the Jews in Russia. While these data are not up-to-date and are incomplete, they remain the best that may be had. Reports were made for only 3,186 out of 7,750 factories existing in the Pale in 1897. In the factories reported for northwestern, southwestern, and southern (new)

Russia 33,933 Jewish factory workers were employed, and in those reported for Poland 12,380 were employed, a total of 46,313 in the factories reported for the Pale.

There can be no doubt that this total is far below the actual number, and an effort may be made to correct the returns of this private investigation, at least approximately, by making the legitimate assumption that in the factories omitted the percentage of Jewish workingmen was the same as in the factories reported, which gives the following:

ESTIMATED NUMBER OF JEWISH WORKINGMEN IN THREE SPECIFIED REGIONS OF THE PALE.

Region.	Number of workingmen.			Per cent of Jewish of total reported to committee.	Calculated number of Jewish working- men.
	According to census figures (1897).	Reported to Jewish colonization committee.			
		Total.	Jewish.		
Northwestern Russia	51,659	41,589	22,279	53.6	27,689
Southwestern Russia	108,769	83,280	9,596	11.5	12,508
Southern (new) Russia	74,775	33,341	2,058	6.2	4,636
Total	235,203	158,210	33,933	21.4	50,033

No such comparison is possible for the 10 Polish Provinces; but if it be supposed that the proportion is about the same and the 12,380 recorded Jewish workingmen of Poland be taken to represent about 18,000 workingmen in that section, then the total number of Jewish factory workers in the entire Pale would be about 68,000. When it is remembered that the large industrial centers like Lodz and Bialystok are included in this total, its inadequacy becomes apparent. It must be borne in mind that these data at best are over nine years old; that, as was shown in a preceding table, the number of factory workers increased 150 per cent in the eight years, 1889 to 1897, and that Russian industry has developed considerably since the latter date. Then, too, it has been pointed out in a previous section of this article that a great number of the so-called artisans' shops are in reality small factories, therefore a considerable number of so-called artisans are but skilled factory employees. When all these facts are taken into consideration, the statement seems plausible that there are at the present time from 100,000 to 150,000 Jewish factory employees in the Pale. It is nevertheless true that while the Jews constitute almost one-half of the city population, and the commercial and industrial half, only about 20 per cent of the factory workers are Jews. A great many reasons, besides those of a historical nature mentioned above, have combined to retard the transformation of the poor Jewish mass in Russia into an army of factory employees; it is because some of these reasons are absent and the others are weakened that this transformation is going on much more rapidly in the United States.

One of these reasons is the strength of the religious convictions of the Russian Jew and his strict compliance with all the rites and observances, especially those relating to the Sabbath. This makes the operating of a factory that employs both Jewish and non-Jewish workingmen a rather difficult matter, because the Jewish workingmen are forced to stop their work at sunset on Friday night and rest on Saturday, while the non-Jewish rest on Sunday. This difficulty becomes more serious in establishments with mechanical power, since neither the plan of running two days a week on half power nor that of stopping work altogether for two days a week is likely to appeal to the manufacturer. The objection to factory work is much stronger among the older than among the younger generation and is rapidly losing ground; but it is still much stronger among the Jews in Russia than among the Jews in New York City, where many factors tend to destroy the strict observance of all demands of the Jewish Church.

Another factor over which the Jews have had no control are the rules regarding the right of sojourn beyond the limits of the cities. It is shown above how these rules keep back Jewish capital from entering various branches of industry. In the case of the Jewish workingman, this entirely prevents employment in some of the important factory industries. Jewish labor is practically unknown in the sugar-beet factories, nearly all of which are located beyond the city limits. In all such factories there were employed only 531 Jewish workingmen out of a total of 65,258, or 0.8 per cent. In lumber mills there were 1,213 Jewish workingmen out of a total of 19,239, or 6.3 per cent. Few Jewish workers were found in the large mining industries.

Another peculiar difficulty that the Jewish workingman is forced to meet when in quest of employment is the strong anti-Semitic sentiment existing among many manufacturers, especially among the manufacturers of Lodz, where German capital is strongly represented. This is shown in the following comparison for 1,867 factories reported in Poland:

TOTAL EMPLOYEES AND NUMBER OF JEWISH EMPLOYEES IN 1,867 FACTORIES IN POLAND, BY OWNERSHIP OF FACTORIES, 1898.

Ownership of factories.	Employees.		
	Total.	Jewish.	Per cent of Jewish of total.
Jewish	43,011	11,954	27.8
Non-Jewish	45,925	426	.9

Though the Jew is much more predominant in the textile factories of Bialystok, the same tendency is noticed there.

TOTAL EMPLOYEES AND NUMBER OF JEWISH EMPLOYEES IN TEXTILE FACTORIES OF BIALYSTOK, BY OWNERSHIP OF FACTORIES, 1898.

Ownership of factories.	Employees.		
	Total.	Jewish.	Per cent of Jewish of total.
Jewish	3,863	2,885	74.7
Non-Jewish	3,908	134	3.4

These figures convey the strong impression that there is a decided racial discrimination in the matter of hiring labor. To some extent it may be explained by the difficulty of the Sabbath rest, which may seem much more objectionable to a non-Jewish than to a Jewish manufacturer. This consideration does not change the economic aspect of the fact that the nationality of the manufacturer becomes a matter of serious import to the workingman. If the newly arrived Jewish immigrant finds no great difficulty in obtaining employment in New York City, it may to a great extent be due to the existence of a large number of Jewish employers, and here may be found the true explanation of at least one important cause of the concentration of the Jewish immigrants in a few large industrial centers.

Strange as it is this racial discrimination may be found in some of the great cotton factories of Lodz, which belong to Jews but are supervised by German master mechanics and foremen who have brought the anti-Semitic feeling along with them from Germany.

Another peculiar reason that works against the Jewish factory worker is the unwillingness to trust him with complicated machinery and mechanical power. There is a decided difference recorded in the proportion of Jewish workingmen as between factories with and factories without mechanical power, the difference being greatest in Poland where the supply of German skilled labor comes in competition with Jewish labor.

TOTAL EMPLOYEES AND NUMBER OF JEWISH EMPLOYEES IN POLISH FACTORIES, CLASSIFIED AS TO WHETHER OR NOT POWER IS USED, 1898.

Kind of factory.	Employees.		
	Total.	Jewish.	Per cent of Jewish of total.
All Poland:			
With power	27,582	5,236	19.0
Without power	15,429	6,718	43.5
Lodz (textile industry):			
With power	10,967	1,184	10.8
Without power	1,881	779	41.4

This distrust probably acts most powerfully in eliminating the Jewish workingman from certain industries, as, for instance, the metal industries and the production of machinery. It may be that the lower muscular strength of the average Jew or his peculiar school training, which lasts through many hours day in and day out for many years and develops his speculative power at the expense of his manual dexterity, makes him unfit for work at many of the machines. Surely it is difficult to suspect the Jew of unwillingness to enter the industries mentioned, when he is usually found in the trades that are most unwholesome and injurious.

The general statistics of occupation may give some information as to the trades preferred by the Jews, but owing to incomplete classification it is impossible to arrive at any definite idea in regard to the kind of factories in which Jewish labor is preferred. The report of the Jewish Colonization Society contains the following table, but unfortunately does not give the actual figures upon which the percentages are based:

PER CENT OF JEWISH EMPLOYEES OF TOTAL EMPLOYEES IN THE PALE IN EACH SPECIFIED INDUSTRY, BY REGIONS, 1898.

Industry.	North-western Russia.	South-western Russia.	Southern (new) Russia.
Gloves	100.0	100.0	
Brushes, etc	96.8		
Matches	95.2	12.0	
Tobacco	92.1	78.4	56.4
Soap	84.7	81.1	63.6
Buttons	84.2		
Hides and tanning	64.6	45.8	68.0
Candies	62.4	100.0	
Wool spinning	57.7		
Flour milling	51.5	34.6	27.3
Beer brewing	50.1	36.5	34.8
Brickmaking	49.4	8.5	3.0
Wool weaving	31.8		
Distilling	25.4	4.2	21.4
Lumber mills	18.3	18.3	30.1
Cast-iron mills	14.9	15.2	.7
Machinery	4.2		

In Poland the data refer to the Jewish factories alone, and such calculation of the percentages would be misleading; but there also the same trades have especially attracted Jewish labor. The textiles employ about 4,000 persons; tobacco, 1,300; paper, about 1,000. It is impossible to escape the conclusion that as yet the most injurious trades continue to monopolize Jewish factory labor, and this tendency is most pronounced in the northwestern Provinces, where the distress is most acute.

FEMALE AND CHILD LABOR IN THE FACTORIES.

In the section devoted to the artisans it is shown that though female work in the industrial field is still a novelty, yet within the last few decades it has been growing more common. It is to be expected that this growth will show itself in a greater degree in factories than in small artisans' shops, for factory work does not as a rule require the same amount of special training. It might be thought that in view of the cheapness of labor the incentive to employ female and child labor would not be strong; but the data in regard to the Jews in the Pale show the fallacy of the assertion that only dearness or scarcity of labor drives the manufacturer to employ female and child labor.

NUMBER AND PER CENT OF JEWISH MEN, WOMEN, BOYS, AND GIRLS IN THE PALE WORKING IN FACTORIES, BY REGIONS, 1898.

Sex.	Northwestern Russia.		Southwestern Russia.		Southern (new) Russia.		Poland.	
	Number.	Per cent.	Number.	Per cent.	Number.	Per cent.	Number.	Per cent.
Men	11,693	57.6	6,746	70.7	1,642	79.8	6,984	62.6
Women	5,492	27.0	988	10.4	106	5.1	2,345	21.0
Boys	1,389	6.8	860	9.0	158	7.7	867	7.8
Girls	1,749	8.6	940	9.9	152	7.4	962	8.6
Total	20,323	100.0	9,534	100.0	2,058	100.0	11,158	100.0

The proportion of female and child labor together is seen to be in indirect proportion to the general level of prosperity. It equals 42.4 per cent in northwestern Russia, 37.4 per cent in Poland, 29.3 per cent in southwestern Russia, and only 20.2 per cent in southern Russia, the four main divisions of the Pale being mentioned in the regular scale of economic well-being.

Female and child labor is found in many industries where its application is likely to be the most injurious—in brick factories, in match factories, in textile factories, etc.—and is encouraged by the development of that most pernicious form of industrial work, the domestic system. Thus, in many small towns where match factories have been established, it is customary for girls to do at home work of a nature that can be done there; such as, for instance, packing the matches. In the textile centers of Lodz and Bialystok there exist a great number of weavers who do their work at home on their own looms, usually all the members of the family taking part in the work, though sometimes they are assisted by a hired worker. This feature of industry has been spoken of above in discussing the marketing of products.

WAGES OF FACTORY WORKERS.

Of the conditions of the wage contract those that are of greatest importance are the hours of work and the wages, and of neither of these two problems is it possible to present accurate statistics; that is, properly calculated averages. The best that can be done is to give all available, fragmentary information, which, though it lacks the desirable scientific accuracy, nevertheless conveys some information as to the general level of wages. Of the hours of work and the organized efforts toward their reduction, an account will be given in the section devoted to the labor movement and the Bund, the main organization of the Jewish wageworkers.

Twenty years ago a Russian economist, Mr. A. P. Subbotin, whose work has already been quoted, investigated the economic condition of the Jewish Pale, and stated that the wages of the factory workers, the number of whom was very small at that time, were "quite high." In the tobacco factories of Vilna they reached as much as 5 rubles ($2.58) per week for the men and 2½ rubles ($1.29) per week for the women. He commended the Jewish workers, because "one never hears of acute conflicts with the employers, which are becoming so common in the central Provinces of Russia." The next section of this article will show how much these conditions have changed within the last twenty years. In the city of Bialystok, which even at that time had begun to gain great importance as a center of the woolen industry, the best paid workingmen, the weavers, sometimes earned from 6 to 8 rubles ($3.09 to $4.12) a week, and this income made the Bialystok weaver an aristocrat among the Jewish workingmen. A great number of children worked in the tobacco factories, where they earned from 25 copecks to 1 ruble (13 to 51.5 cents) a week.

Of all the Jewish wageworkers the brush makers are the best organized. As early as 1895 they succeeded in forming a general union of the brush workers, which in 1897 joined the Bund as an independent national union. In its report to the international socialist congress in Paris in 1900 this union contributed a table of wages of brush makers in the twelve main towns of the Pale. From this table the following data are taken: ([a])

The average weekly wages in different towns varied from 2.80 to 5.85 rubles ($1.44 to $3.01), the maximum ranging from 5 to 8 rubles ($2.58 to $4.12) and the minimum from 5.25 rubles to 75 copecks ($2.70 to 39 cents). Even this income was not steady, because the number of weeks of regular employment during a year varied from 46 to 25.

In the two large volumes on the economic condition of the Jews in Russia, published by the St. Petersburg committee of the Jewish Colonization Society, very little information in regard to wages is to be found, because the data were collected from the proprietors of the factories, and it was feared that a question in regard to wages would prevent a truthful answer to all questions asked. The few fragmentary data found therein refer to 1897, and therefore may not have more than a theoretical value. In Warsaw, in the metal industry, the Jewish workers at that time did not earn more than 30 to 35

[a] Zhisn, a Russian magazine which was published for a short time in London, June, 1902, p. 83.

copecks (15 to 18 cents) per day, on the average, the maximum being
about 1 ruble (51.5 cents) for the men and 70 copecks (36 cents) for
the women. In a trade as skilled as that of a clockmaker the weekly
wages of adults were only from 7 to 15 rubles ($3.61 to $7.73) and
those of children from 2 to 4 rubles ($1.03 to $2.06). In the toy
factories in Czenstochow, Poland, the wages of adult Jewish workers
were stated to be from 3 to 5 rubles ($1.55 to $2.58) per week, while
girls below 15 years of age, who made up 60 per cent of the employees,
received from 80 copecks to 1.20 rubles (41 to 62 cents) and those
over 15 years from 1.80 rubles to 2.50 rubles (93 cents to $1.29) a
week. In Lodz the weavers who are in the employ of the factories,
but who do their work at home, earn from 8 to 10 rubles ($4.12 to
$5.15) a week, but they usually employ help, whose earnings seldom
exceed 3 or 4 rubles ($1.55 to $2.06). In the woolen factories of
Bialystok the weekly wages of the male workers seldom exceed 6
rubles ($3.09), while those of the women and girls are as low as 1.50
or 2 rubles (77 cents or $1.03).

It is probable that down to the second half of the nineties the
average wages of the Jewish workers did not rise much, if at all. The
growing congestion of the cities of the Pale and the increase of special
restrictive legislation against the Jews so flooded the labor market
that natural competition was all against the wageworkers. From
that time on, however, the Jewish labor movement has asserted itself,
and while the general level of wages remains low from the European
and especially from the American point of view, the present conditions seem to indicate a strong tendency toward increased wages.
The official publications of the Bund, which formerly appeared in
Geneva, contained in nearly every number accounts of strikes, usually very small ones, where the demands for both shortening of the
labor day and for increase of wages were invariably made and often
carried. Unfortunately the correspondents cared a great deal more
for the political effects than for the economic results of the strikes, and
seldom reported the actual wages and the increases. From private
inquiries made of many persons who recently left the Jewish Pale
and had either worked in the factories or had the opportunity to
observe the life of Jewish workers it seems a warrantable conclusion
that 6 or 8 rubles ($3.09 or $4.12) a week is a very fair wage and
that the ordinary wage is probably nearer to 5 rubles ($2.58).

LABOR ORGANIZATIONS.

The organization mentioned several times in the preceding pages
as having influenced the conditions of work of the Jewish wageworker
in Russia is the so-called Bund, or to use its official title, "Der allge-
meine Jüdische Arbeiterbund in Littauen, Polen, und Russland."

The economic activity of the Bund is all that concerns us here, but it is difficult, if not impossible, to understand this interesting organization without a few remarks with regard to its general nature, which is a peculiar one, owing to the exceptional political conditions of Russia. In its economic field the Bund endeavors to do the work of the American labor unions, yet it is a very different organization from the American Federation of Labor.

It must be borne in mind that the Russian code does not provide for the existence of labor unions, and that even at the present time, when dozens of labor unions have been formed in the open since October, 1905, a law providing for the existence of such organizations is still in the process of elaboration. Also, it must be remembered that Russian law specifically prohibits the strike, the main weapon of a labor union, as well as any form of collective activity. Thus, every effort at labor organization and collective bargaining is legally a crime, and this prevents the growth of a peaceful labor movement. The low educational standard of the mass of the workingmen is another great obstacle to such development. In discussing the "khevras" in a preceding section it was shown how out of these mutual benefit organizations of the Jewish artisans, whose educational and intellectual standard fifteen or twenty years ago was immeasurably higher than that of the Russian workingmen, some semblance of a limited labor movement developed; but these secret and local organizations could not have any great influence over the condition of the working class.

Both the Jewish and the Russian labor movements have grown out of the political revolutionary propaganda and are still closely associated with it.

During the nine or ten years of its existence the history of the Bund, notwithstanding the great obstacles which the necessity of secrecy put in the way of a labor movement, was one of very rapid growth. According to the report presented by the central committee of the Bund to the International Socialist Congress, held in Amsterdam in 1904, the number of organized workingmen in 1904 was estimated to be 30,000, (a) but any such estimate may have only a general value. Undoubtedly a great many persons must be under the influence of this organization who do not wish to be openly identified with it. Then, too, in hundreds of small towns clubs have been established which are not always in direct communication with the central organization. In the same report 35 large and important cities are mentioned in which organizations of the Bund existed, but the periodical publications of the Bund often contribute news of the activity

---

a Die Thätigkeit des Allgemeinen Jüdischen Arbeiterbundes in Littauen, Polen, und Russland ("Bund") nach Seinem V. Parteitag. Geneva, 1904.

of the Bund organizations beyond these 35 cities. Thus, within that year alone over 25,000 Jewish workingmen struck in the region influenced by the Bund, and in the general strike which swept over Russia during the second half of the year 1905 the number of Jewish strikers went into hundreds of thousands.

This origin of the Jewish labor movement in the socialist and revolutionary movement had very significant consequences, since it led to a close union of efforts: Of the working masses to improve their economic condition; of the Jewish race in Russia to improve its legal standing, and of the revolutionary elements to introduce an entirely different form of government in the Russian Empire. The distinctive feature of the Bund is that it endeavors to do all these things at the same time, and to a certain extent other Russian socialist organizations share this peculiarity with the Bund.

A few data as to the extent of the activity of the Bund will be found suggestive. According to the imperfect registry kept by the central committee of the Bund, there took place during the year, June, 1903, to June, 1904, 429 meetings, in 418 of which 74,162 persons participated; 45 street demonstrations, in 31 of which 20,340 persons took part, and 41 political strikes (including 35 May celebrations), in 31 of which there were 23,035 participants.

The term "political strike" is used when a stoppage of work is ordered by the organization for no specific economic reason, but simply to demonstrate the strength of the movement. Such strikes are usually of brief duration, being ordered for only one, two, or three days, as the case may be. They are especially frequent on the 1st of May, all socialist organizations in Russia celebrating that day with short strikes or with street demonstrations and large meetings.

During the same year 109 strikes were reported, and in 101 of these strikes, for which careful data were furnished, 24,124 person participated.

The strikes are usually conducted by the local organizations of the Bund, together with the assistance of the strikers themselves although among the strikers many men are often found who are no permanently identified with the organization. In preparation fo such a strike the workingmen of a certain industry or trade, or eve of a certain factory, may combine and keep up some form of benefi fund, but this is far from being a trade union. One of the man interesting features of the Jewish labor movement is the fact tha although the central committees of the Bund made every effort t keep up among the workingmen the agitation for strikes and othe forms of struggle with the employers, they did not encourage th formation of trade unions; not because they doubted the econom efficacy of the trade union in the work of improving the condition the workingmen, but because, so they claimed, the formation of trad unions would narrow down the efforts of the workingmen to their own individual or group interests, and thus deplete the ranks of the fighters for the political cause. The leaders themselves feel that such a policy, aside from its wisdom or unwisdom, can not be carried on when the formation of labor unions shall have been legalized in Russia. Even at the present time the project of a law to legalize unions and strikes is being actively elaborated in St. Petersburg. Immediately after the issuance of the manifesto of October 17 (29), 1905, dozens of labor unions were formed within as well as without the Pale. The question of the attitude of the Bund, as a political organization, toward the formation of these unions immediately arose, and the decision reached is significant.

In the official circular published in the last -issue of the Letzte Nachrichten (No. 255), dated December, 1905, the central committee of the Bund calls attention to the fact that the conditions caused by the manifesto of October 17 (29), 1905, make the creation of professional (trade) unions, both possible and necessary.

According to Mr. M. Gourevitsch, who is a member of the central committee of the Bund, the economic activity of the Bund is becoming greater each day. The period 1897 to 1900 was one of struggle for a 10-hour labor day (or twelve hours a day with two hours at midday for rest). At present the struggle may be characterized as one for the 9 and 8 hour day in the higher trades and the larger cities, and a 10-hour day in the small towns and lower trades. The strikes for this shortening of the labor day have had unusual success. Out of the 119 strikes which were registered in the year 1903–4, 81, or 68 per cent, ended in a full victory for the workingmen; 23, or 19 per cent, in partial victory for the workingmen, and 15, or 13 per cent, in failures. Approximately, of the victorious strikes 50 per cent led to the establishment of a 10½-hour (or 10 hours net) day, 30 per cent to a 9-hour day, 10 per cent to an 8-hour day, and 10 per cent to a 11-hour day. While the shortening through each strike is usually equal to 1 hour, sometimes in very backward trades much more considerable reductions have taken place at once. The female bakers within the last few years have succeeded in reducing their hours of work from 19 to 12; the tailors, from 17 to 12; the shoemakers, from 17 to 12, and, as will be pointed out elsewhere, the salesmen, from 15 or 16 to 10 or 11. In the latter half of the year 1904 there were registered 56 strikes, of which number 41 were defensive and 15 offensive. Of these 56 strikes, about 70 per cent were successful. An interesting feature of the activity of the Bund within recent times is the carrying of the agitation for strikes among those classes of employees in which neither the United Kingdom nor the United States have been used to see any organized efforts for the improving of the conditions of the wage contracts. Of the strikes of the commercial employees more will be said when discussing the condition of that class. Draymen in Pinsk and Berdichev, boatmen in Kovno, hotel attendants in Pinsk and Slonim, and even domestic servants in Warsaw, Grodno, Moheelev, Bobruisk, Pinsk, and Dvinsk have struck for higher wages and shorter hours. Strangely enough the domestic servants have shown themselves especially susceptible to the agitation of the Bund. The following, for instance, were the conditions demanded by the servants during their strike in Dvinsk:

Hours to be from 8 a. m. to 9 p. m., with a recess of one and one-half hours.
On Saturdays the work shall stop at 3 p. m.
Wages to be increased.
The servants to have private rooms.
The employer to provide medical treatment in case of necessity.
The right to receive visitors after working hours.
In case of dismissal without cause the servant shall receive two weeks' salary.

The many-sided activity of the Bund, carried on as it was until recently under conditions of great secrecy, did not offer many opportunities for development of original methods of trade-union activity. As has been shown, its activity was mainly in the nature of strikes. Only occasionally were boycotts used, and then almost exclusively for causes which were not purely economic. The Bundists take the ground that the law is against the workingmen, and that the rules of a fair fight forbid the employer from appealing too readily to the police and the military for assistance. Moreover, where striking workingmen have been turned over by their employers to the authorities the strikers have been punished not so much for participation in the strike as for belonging to the revolutionary Bund. Such appeals are therefore considered in the nature of informing and are punished by declaration of a boycott. The best known case is that of a shoe manufacturer in Warsaw against whom a boycott was declared soon after the strike wave of January, 1905. The boycott must have threatened him with ruin, since the manufacturer was forced to appeal to the Bund for relief, promising to yield to all their demands. The boycott against him was called off only after he sent the following declaration to the local committee of the Bund in Warsaw, which declaration was published in full in the official organ of the Bund: ([a])

DECLARATION.

Recognizing that the boycott declared against me by the Bund for my contemptible treatment of my workingmen (as physical assault, and even turning them over into the hands of the police) has been well deserved by me; recognizing that I am actually guilty of the accusations brought against me, and desiring to clear my name of

[a] Die Letzte Nachrichten, No. 244; August 5, 1905.

this disgraceful blot, I applied to the Warsaw committee of the Bund with the request to call off the boycott against me, and agreed in advance to all the demands which will be made by the Bund.

These demands are as follows: To dismiss several objectionable workingmen; to reimburse the workingmen for all the time during which they were out of employment through my fault; not to give out any work to be performed in the house of the workingmen; to employ only those workingmen who will be indicated by the Bund; and to publish all these facts in some newspaper.

(Signed)   ——— ———.

Warsaw, June 23, 1905.

Only a very disastrous boycott could call forth such a statement; and this effectiveness of the boycott is due to the fact that the influence of the Bund extends beyond the workingmen far into the middle classes, among those who are willing to disregard the economic work of the Bund on account of its political work and its defense of the Jew.

COMMERCIAL PURSUITS.

While the general impression that the Russian Jew is a person fit only for commercial life has been shown to be at variance with the facts, it remains true that commerce employs a great number of the Jewish breadwinners in Russia. According to the Russian census, as shown in the table on page —, 31.6 per cent of the Jews employed in gainful occupations were earning their living from some form of commerce. If, in addition to these persons, the number dependent upon them for a livelihood is considered, it appears that 35.6 per cent of the total Jewish population in Russia belong to the commercial class. In calculating these per cents the hotel, restaurant, and saloon keepers have been omitted from the commercial class in order to conform the classification to that of the United States census. If these occupations with their dependents are included under commerce the percentage in the commercial class rises to 37.5 per cent of all the Jews in Russia. Therefore, a study of Jewish commerce is a matter of utmost importance. It is to be regretted, however, that very little authentic data in regard to this subject are to be had, the only available data being more than 20 years old, and for that reason scarcely applicable at this time. But while accurate statistical data are lacking, that does not preclude the possibility of drawing a more or less true picture of the condition of the Jewish merchants.

According to the Russian census of 1897, a total of 1,495,087 persons were employed in commercial pursuits in all Russia (including hotel and liquor saloon keepers). Of this total the Jews number 474,833 persons, or 31.8 per cent. But in the Pale the proportion is considerably greater. As is shown in the following table, the Jews constitute nearly three-fourths of the commercial class of the Pale (448,514 out of 618,762, or 72.5 per cent). This proportion between the number of Jews and the total number of persons engaged in commercial pursuits varies considerably from region to region and from one Province to another. In the northwest the Jews constitute almost 90 per cent of the commercial class—in Grodno and in Minsk even over 92 per cent. Practically all the commercial activity in these Provinces is in the hands of the Jews. In the southwest the Jews constitute only three-fourths of the commercial class, and in southern (new) Russia a little over one-half. The percentage rapidly declines the farther we go from the center of Jewish congestion, which is found in the northwest; and with the decline of this percentage there was noticeable, at least until the recent disturbances, a rise in the economic condition of the merchants.

The following table gives by Provinces and by regions in the Pale the number of Jews engaged in commerce compared with the total number of persons so engaged:

NUMBER OF JEWS ENGAGED IN COMMERCE COMPARED WITH TOTAL PERSONS SO ENGAGED IN THE PALE, BY PROVINCES AND REGIONS, 1897.

Compiled from the separate reports in Provinces of Premier Recensement Général de la Population de l'Empire de Russie, 1897.]

Province and region.	Total persons engaged in commerce.(a)	Jews engaged in commerce.(a)	
		Number.	Per cent of total.
Vilna	18,884	16,178	85.7
Grodno	20,545	19,005	92.5
Kovno	20,662	17,821	86.3
Lithuania	60,091	53,004	88.2
Minsk	25,555	23,588	92.3
Vitebsk	19,781	16,713	84.5
Moheelev	19,578	17,641	90.1
White Russia	64,914	57,942	89.3
Volhynia	39,434	35,172	89.2
Podolia	44,660	39,040	87.4
Kiev	63,740	45,718	71.7
Chernigov	21,015	12,736	60.6
Poltava	23,954	13,910	58.1
Southwestern Russia	192,803	146,576	76.0
Bessarabia	32,253	24,636	76.4
Kherson	62,321	37,058	59.5
Yekaterinoslav	25,823	11,673	45.2
Taurida	25,385	5,987	23.6
Southern (new) Russia	145,782	79,354	54.4
Warsaw	52,497	32,178	61.3
Kalisz	9,305	5,995	64.4
Kielce	10,240	8,725	85.2
Lomza	6,477	5,484	84.7
Lublin	16,019	13,982	87.3
Petrikau	28,812	19,860	68.9
Plock	5,810	2,579	44.4
Radom	11,313	9,946	87.9
Suvalki	4,987	4,169	83.6
Siedlec	9,712	8,720	89.8
Poland	155,172	111,638	71.9
Total in Pale(a)	a 618,762	a 448,514	72.5

a Including hotel, restaurant, and saloon keepers; hence totals do not agree with totals shown for commerce in tables on pages 501 and 502.

In a preceding section a table was given (p. 502), showing the distribution of the Jews gainfully employed into the great occupation groups by separate regions of the Pale. It was shown there that of all Jews engaged in gainful occupations a smaller percentage were in commercial life in the northwest than in the south and southwest. On the other hand, we find here that of all persons engaged in commerce the Jews constitute a larger proportion in the northwest than in the south. Coupled with the fact that the south received most of its Jewish population by immigration from the northwest, these percentages seem to indicate that, until recently at least, southern Russia offered better prospects to Jewish immigrants of the middle classes, while the wage-earners were tending to the New World.

An analysis of the proportion of the Jews in various branches of commercial life presents many interesting features. It shows, first of all, that almost one-half of all the Jewish merchants deal in agricultural products such as cattle, grain, hides, furs, etc. It also shows a very high proportion of that trade in Jewish hands. Thus over 90 per cent of the grain dealers' are Jews—in southwestern Russia as high as 96.7 per cent and in Lithuania 97.1 per cent. A very large number of Jews is found in general commerce or the group of commercial middlemen and peddlers, which usually means very petty trading. The better paying branches of commercial activity are just those in which the number of Jews is smallest. Thus institutions of credit require some capital, and the Jews constitute only 34.9 per cent of that class in the Pale, while in the south they constitute only 29.1 and in Poland only 18.1 per cent. A bookstore can not be opened without special permission, and as a result less than half of the stores of that group are in Jewish hands. Of the liquor saloon keepers, less than two-fifths and of the hotel keepers less than one-third are Jews. In the southwest the number of Jews employed as liquor saloon keepers is extremely small.

NUMBER OF JEWS ENGAGED IN COMMERCE COMPARED WITH TOTAL PERSONS SO ENGAGED IN THE PALE, BY MERCANTILE PURSUITS AND REGIONS, 1897.

[Compiled from separate reports on Provinces of Premier Recensement Général de la Population de l'Empire de Russie, 1897.]

Mercantile pursuits.	Lithuania.			White Russia.			Southwestern Russia.		
	Total per- sons.	Jews.		Total per- sons.	Jews.		Total per- sons.	Jews.	
		Num- ber.	Per cent of total.		Num- ber.	Per cent of total.		Num- ber.	Per cent of total.
Institutions of credit	797	416	52.2	579	365	63.0	1,783	690	38.7
Commercial middlemen	1,255	1,116	88.9	1,478	1,341	90.7	5,173	4,499	87.0
General commerce	10,607	9,714	91.6	9,591	8,790	91.6	35,487	29,113	82.0
Dealers in—									
Cattle	1,388	1,227	88.4	3,230	2,621	81.1	8,793	6,825	77.6
Grain	2,423	2,353	97.1	3,325	3,120	93.8	21,344	20,643	96.7
Other agricultural products	21,817	20,134	92.3	23,784	22,264	93.6	57,549	44,168	76.7
Building material and fuel	3,424	3,192	93.2	6,486	5,950	91.7	11,154	9,538	85.5
Household goods	664	585	88.1	699	605	86.6	2,065	1,878	70.5
Metal goods and machinery	710	611	86.1	836	770	92.1	2,593	2,021	77.9
Dry goods and clothing	4,066	3,799	93.4	4,160	3,980	95.7	14,976	12,802	85.5
Hides, furs, etc	1,401	1,133	80.9	1,578	1,527	96.8	5,583	4,512	80.8
Articles of luxury, books, etc	644	416	64.6	577	467	80.9	1,577	634	40.2
Miscellaneous articles	1,195	822	68.8	1,312	790	60.2	4,034	2,845	70.5
Peddlers, etc	3,321	3,090	93.0	2,077	1,769	85.2	3,825	2,200	57.5
Hotel and restaurant keepers	2,794	1,453	52.0	2,545	1,555	61.1	7,757	3,377	43.5
Liquor saloon keepers, etc	3,585	2,943	82.1	2,657	2,028	76.3	8,510	831	9.8
Total	60,091	53,004	88.2	64,914	57,942	89.3	192,803	146,576	76.0

Mercantile pursuits.	Southern Russia.			Poland.			Pale.		
	Total per- sons.	Jews.		Total per- sons.	Jews.		Total per- sons.	Jews.	
		Num- ber.	Per cent of total.		Num- ber.	Per cent of total.		Num- ber.	Per cent of total.
Institutions of credit	1,608	468	29.1	1,622	293	18.1	6,389	2,232	34.9
Commercial middlemen	5,726	4,103	71.7	5,870	4,185	71.3	19,502	15,244	78.2
General commerce	18,897	10,479	55.5	42,337	32,083	75.8	116,919	90,179	77.1
Dealers in—									
Cattle	3,254	1,774	54.5	3,885	3,001	77.2	20,550	15,448	75.2
Grain	17,596	14,041	79.9	8,056	7,350	91.2	52,744	47,507	90.1
Other agricultural products	42,978	22,865	53.2	40,059	28,776	71.8	186,187	138,207	74.2
Building material and fuel	5,942	3,725	62.7	5,328	3,915	73.5	32,334	26,320	81.4
Household goods	2,234	1,279	57.3	1,494	1,200	80.3	7,756	5,547	71.5
Metal goods and machinery	2,067	1,318	63.8	2,133	1,747	81.9	8,339	6,467	77.6
Dry goods and clothing	16,025	10,599	66.1	10,534	8,541	81.1	49,761	39,721	79.8
Hides, furs, etc	2,511	1,671	66.5	3,416	3,039	89.0	14,489	11,882	82.0
Articles of luxury, books, etc	1,333	516	38.7	1,650	790	47.9	5,781	2,823	48.8
Miscellaneous articles	2,996	1,283	42.8	2,431	1,548	63.7	11,968	7,288	60.9
Peddlers, etc	4,251	2,030	47.8	9,893	8,674	87.7	23,367	17,763	76.0
Hotel and restaurant keepers	11,149	1,899	17.0	6,171	1,679	27.2	30,416	9,963	32.8
Liquor saloon keepers, etc	7,215	1,304	18.1	10,293	4,817	46.8	32,260	11,923	37.0
Total	145,782	79,354	54.4	155,172	111,638	71.9	a618,762	a448,514	72.5

a These totals do not agree with those given under commerce in the tables on pages 501 and 502, where the hotel, restaurant, and saloon keepers are included in personal service.

Of the total number of Jewish merchants in the Pale, 213,044, or 47.5 per cent, were dealing in agricultural products (including hides, furs, etc.). Their function evidently is to gather the farm products from the agricultural population of the Pale for shipment and sale in distant localities, and they stand to the surrounding population in the capacity of buyers. With the exception of small groups of large wholesale merchants the majority of the remaining 52.5 per cent are sellers of various kinds of goods to the same population of the villages, and also to the population of the cities. It is a fallacy of old standing that the only occupation of the Jew of the Pale is to sell liquor to the Russian peasant. No matter what the wishes of the average Jew might have been in the matter, it is an important fact that in 1897 only 32.8 per cent of the hotel and restaurant keepers and only 37.0 per cent of the liquor-saloon keepers were Jews. Undoubtedly this was in a measure due to the legislative restrictions, the laws of 1882 having forced many Jews out of the liquor business by denying them the right to live in the villages. Another factor of no less importance was the introduction of the State monopoly of the sale of liquor. The effect of this measure is only partly reflected in the statistics of 1897, because the census was taken during the time of the gradual introduction of this measure in the Pale. As a result, the proportion of Jewish saloon keepers in southwestern Russia was only 9.8 per cent and in the south 18.1 per cent, while in the northwest nearly 80 per cent of the saloon keepers were Jews. Since then practically all the Jews have been eliminated from this field of commerce, and doubtless the families (nearly 12,000) that lived by this trade in 1897 were forced to swell the army of the unemployed in the cities.

In this connection it is worthy of notice that under conditions of freedom to enter the saloon keeper's trade the Russian Jews do not show any strong liking for this occupation. As is shown in the following table, the male Russians gainfully employed in New York City constitute 6.56 per cent of all male persons gainfully employed, while the Russian saloon keepers represent only 2.77 per cent of the total number of saloon keepers. In other words, while there are 45 saloon keepers per 10,000 males gainfully employed there are only 19 Russian saloon keepers per 10,000 Russians gainfully employed as against 56 per 10,000 in the remaining foreign population. The mass of the Jewish merchants and all persons occupied in some commercial activity, whether or not they deserve to be called merchants, may be classified into two groups—those who stand toward the local population in the capacity of buyers and those who are sellers of goods. The buyers are those who come mostly in contact with the agricultural population. It is this class which is probably meant where the report of the census of 1897 says: "The Jews do not till the land themselves, but exploit the land tiller." In view of this official opinion it is interesting to study the methods which are used by these buyers in dealing with the peasants.

NUMBER AND PER CENT OF RUSSIAN MALES AND OF MALES IN OTHER NATIVITY GROUPS ENGAGED IN ALL GAINFUL OCCUPATIONS AND AS SALOON KEEPERS IN NEW YORK CITY, AND NUMBER OF SALOON KEEPERS PER 10,000 MALES EMPLOYED IN EACH GROUP, 1900.

[Compiled from report on Occupations: Twelfth Census of the United States, pages 635 and 636.]

Nativity.	Males employed.		Male saloon keepers.		Number of saloon keepers per 10,000 males employed.
	Number.	Per cent.	Number.	Per cent.	
Russians	72,291	6.56	136	2.77	19
All other foreign white and native white of foreign parentage.	808,307	73.31	4,514	91.88	56
Native white of native parentage	195,205	17.71	236	4.80	12
Colored	26,668	2.42	27	.55	10
Total	1,102,471	100.00	4,913	100.00	45

The 213,044 dealers in agricultural products serve in the movement of the crops and other agricultural products from the peasant to the market, which is usually some distance away, and often beyond the borders of Russia. In estimating this function it must be remembered that the commercial methods of the Russian peasants are exceedingly primitive; there are no local elevators and no feeding railroad lines, and the peasant, when forced to sell some of his grain so as to pay his taxes and buy the few simple necessaries of life, outside of his food, takes the grain to the market to sell, and in the Pale the buyer in almost nine cases out of ten is the Jew. The Jewish "merchant," whose only capital may be the price of a few bushels of corn, is more anxious to buy than the peasant is to sell, for the latter is sure of his ability to sell all he has, the question being only between a higher or lower price, while the Jew is by far not so sure of his ability to buy, and it is the difference of a few cents more or less that means to him either some profit or a loss. It is therefore the buyer that is anxious to capture the seller, and because he has no legal right to travel from one village to the other buying up grain, and as any such transaction would require considerable capital, he employs on the market day the primitive method of going out as far as possible on the road to intercept the peasant before other buyers reach him. The competition among the buyers is very severe and the Jewish merchant is satisfied with almost any profit. It is true that he has better bargaining ability than the Russian peasant, but it is doubtful whether the peasant could obtain as good prices as he does if this keen competition did not exist. Having bought the few bushels of grain or the small quantities of other agricultural products, the Jew is anxious to sell as quickly as possible, that he may recover his capital, and he sells to a merchant who is in a position to accumulate purchases of a few carloads until he is ready to ship them to the central market or to Germany.

By reason of the peculiar conditions that prevail in Russia the farm products invariably pass through many more hands than they would otherwise have to, but the rate of profit to each is so small that the entire increment is not excessive. Thus the small merchant of this kind runs about the whole day in his effort to buy as much as possible and as cheaply as possible and considers a daily income of from 50 copecks to 1 ruble (25.8 to 51.5 cents) satisfactory. That sum is scarcely sufficient for his modest living, but it is about as large an income as that of the average artisan without any capital or of the average factory worker; and this merchant is a man with little capital and is of the same social scale as the artisan or the factory worker. This is the condition of the great majority of the grain merchants, though above this class there are the important business men of the centers.

A few decades ago this trade in grain and in other articles of agricultural production was a source of prosperity to many little towns in the northwest. Before the construction of railroads the methods of marketing were different, the competition among the buyers was a great deal less acute, the surplus of the peasants was much greater, and the local market was not so sensitive to the changes of the world market. Thirty or forty years ago the Pale used to ship large quantities of grain, eggs, lumber, etc., along the Niemen and other rivers to the German markets. After making sufficient purchases the Jewish grain dealer or lumber dealer went personally on the rafts to the German markets and sold his merchandise at high profits. But the development of the Russian railroad system and the agricultural growth of the Far East so reduced the grain trade of the northwest, and the increase of the local urban population so affected the surplus, that many families which had accumulated small competencies from this branch of commerce found themselves without any means of subsistence and were forced to migrate into larger cities or to the United States. There are dozens of small settlements all along the Niemen which have fallen from a state of comparative prosperity into one of abject poverty. The few large grain merchants who may be found in most Jewish towns do not in any way disturb the truthfulness of this picture. The very fact—pointed out in a previous section—that the number of artisans and factory workers is rapidly growing, notwithstanding the very large emigration, which to a great extent consists of this class, shows that the earnings of the majority of the business men are probably smaller than the earnings of a busy factory worker, and that in spite of the deplorable condition of the shop and factory workers there is a constant stream from the commercial pursuits into the trades and into the factories.

The other large class of merchants are the retail dealers, who are to be found in such large numbers in every town of the Pale. It is more than probable that the data of the census are far from complete, the tendency having been to classify among dependents many members of the family who are in reality employed at some trade, especially if it be the same trade in which the head of the family is occupied. The incomes of the majority of the "grain dealers" are so small that the wives are forced to sell something so as to earn a few cents a day.

While a superficial investigation of the trade in the Pale proves the presence of an unnecessarily great number of middlemen, a closer investigation shows that the sufferers are the middlemen themselves and not the consumers. The cheapness of all articles surprises the stranger, and the purchaser who is not a seller profits considerably thereby; but these advantages can not appeal to the Jew very strongly, because most of the purchasers are themselves sellers, and they suffer a great deal more than they profit by the system. The agricultural population seem to be the positive gainers by this competition, and gainers in a double sense—as producers of agricultural products, for which there is always a brisk demand, and as consumers of articles of manufacture, which they obtain at a comparatively low price. It has been acknowledged by many investigators that the average profit of the Jew on the purchase of grain and like products is much smaller than the profit of the Russian middleman in the interior of Russia in similar transactions, and that the general level of prices on manufactured articles in the cities of the Pale is much lower than in the Russian towns. More than this, it is a matter of common observation that even in the same towns the prices in the Jewish stores are lower than in the Russian stores, for, says Subbotin, "The Jewish merchant is satisfied to receive a smaller rate of profit on his turnover, so long as he can turn his capital quicker."

The same observer during his investigation found that in the Province of Minsk the average rate of profit in the stores of the Jewish merchants was 8.07 per cent, while in the stores of the non-Jewish merchants it was 10.02 per cent. In the Province of Kovno the rate of profit to Jews was 4 per cent, while that to the other merchants was 10 per cent. In Kiev the rates were 4.8 per cent and 5.3 per cent, respectively. In Odessa, where the volume of commerce is much larger, the rates of profit were much lower, namely, 2.6 per cent and 3.1 per cent. That the entrance of the Jew into the grain trade of Odessa has diminished the rate of the middleman's profits is acknowledged by so well known a Russian economist as Professor Yanson.[a]

But Russian evidence of this fact is scarcely necessary, since the same phenomenon has been well observed in the United States wherever Russian Jews have entered commerce, no matter how petty that commerce may be. It may safely be said that nowhere in the United States are the prices of general merchandise, whether it be dry goods, clothing, or groceries of well-known make and supposedly fixed prices, so low in price as they are on the east side of New York City. Any investigation of retail prices in other cities will show the same differences between Jewish and non-Jewish prices.

It has been stated above that this competition has been intensified during the last twenty years because of the rapid growth of the number of Jewish merchants. This is shown by the great number of new licenses which are issued to merchants each year. But not all trading requires such licenses. The most distressing feature of the economic situation of the Pale is the large number of "pauper merchants," if one may use this term. The women peddlers have already been spoken of. There is, however, a large number of small storekeepers whose economic condition is in no way better than that of the peddlers on the streets or in the markets. These "stores" are located in miserable holes, with but little light or air, and with very limited space. All the available goods for sale may not be worth more than 5 rubles ($2.58), empty boxes, bags, and papers being artfully displayed with the intention to deceive the prospective buyer into the belief that the "store" is really a store. How these merchants manage to pay the rent and eke out a living is a mystery that is solved only when the kind of living is known. In these "stores" from early morn until midnight may be seen the storekeeper, usually a woman clothed in rags, patiently waiting for the rare customer.

All this must not be taken to mean that there are no large Jewish commercial houses in the Jewish towns, because it is well known that the origin of some of the fortunes among Russian Jews was due to commerce and not to manufacture. To the Jews belong a number of the better stores in the cities of the Pale, even though the non-Jewish element is much greater in the field of commerce on a larger scale. Not only is the entire commercial class, which, with the children and dependents, numbers almost 2,000,000, far from being economically homogeneous, but within this class an antagonism between the employer and the employee has developed which, though perhaps not so acute, is more extensive than the correspond-

---

[a] See V Cherte Evreiskoy Osedlosti (Within the Jewish Pale), by A. P. Subbotin. St. Petersburg, 1888. Vol. II, p. 218.

ing conflict between the manufacturer and his wageworkers. With the extremely low profit rate and the usually high rent (a result of commercial competition), the profits of the more prosperous merchants in the Pale are derived from two sources, an unusually rapid turning over of the capital and the low expenses of business management, both factors meaning hard work and small pay for the commercial employees.

Unfortunately the basis of the occupation statistics of the Russian census of 1897 has been the nature of the establishment and not the technical or economic quality of the work. It is therefore impossible to tell how many of the 452,193 Jews reported as employed in commerce were salesmen or other employees of the merchants and not independent tradesmen. But the number is undoubtedly large, probably as large as the number of Jewish factory employees.

Until recently the conditions of work of these commercial employees were more onerous than those connected with work in the factories. The small Jewish retail dealer knows no limitations of his working day, the anxiety to find the buyer being so great that the small stores are kept open from 6 or 7 o'clock in the morning till 12 o'clock at night. Until a short time ago this was also the rule in the larger stores, where, besides the members of the family, additional help is employed. Under the influence of the examples of the many successful strikes of the factory and small-shop workers, the commercial employees became restive; but until the end of the last century they had no hope of active resistance, since the abundance of unemployed labor in the market naturally increased the competition in the Pale for even the poorest paid positions. Nevertheless the principle of collective bargaining which the Bund organizations preached with such energy appealed to them as well as to the factory workers. In many cities the initiative of the strikes among the commercial employees came from the labor organizations, while in other cities the salesmen and clerks sought from the more experienced organizations advice and help.

The following detailed account of the salesmen's strike in Kishinev, typical in many respects of the whole, will best characterize the movement: [a]

Kishenev, June 25, O. S.—Under influence of salesmen's strikes in various cities considerable excitement began to manifest itself among our salesmen. A few salesmen made efforts to organize professional salesmen's unions, but we began to appear at their meetings and imbue them with the social democratic spirit. Within seven or eight weeks as many as 60 meetings were called, the attendance at which varied from 10 to 100 men. * * * These meetings caused the development among the salesmen of a very energetic militant spirit. * * *

---

[a] Letzte Nachrichten, No. 244, August 5, 1905.

It was originally intended to call a strike for the beginning of August, when the season begins, but the salesmen themselves hurried us with the declaration of the strike, pointing to the excited condition of the mass of their comrades. * * * It was, therefore, decided to declare the strike immediately. The following demands were formulated:

1. The labor day shall be, April 1 to September 1, from 7 a. m. to 7 p. m., and September 1 to April 1, from 8 a. m. to 8 p. m.

2. The time from 1 to 3 p. m. shall be allowed for dinner, the stores to be closed during the dinner recess.

3. No work from the beginning of a holiday till the next morning after the holiday.(ª)

4. Annual leave of four weeks with pay.

5. Increase of pay.

6. Double monthly salary before the Passover and Succoth [the two most important Jewish holidays].

7. Pay during sickness: In full during the first three months, and half pay during the following three months, the employee to be reinstated after recovery.

8. Payment of the salary on the 1st and the 15th of every month, in advance.

9. The employer must notify his employee of intended dismissal: Those who have been in service less than three years, three months in advance; those having been in service from three to eight years, six months in advance; those having been in service from eight to fifteen years, nine months in advance; and those having been in service more than fifteen years, an entire year in advance.

10. Polite treatment of the employees.

11. The employees shall not be forced to draw customers.

12. The salesmen shall be obliged to perform only those duties which are directly connected with commerce.

13. The right to sit and read when not employed.

14. The salesmen shall not be obliged to deliver purchases to the homes of the customers.

15. The stores shall be heated.

16. The salesmen shall be provided with tea twice a day.

17. The wives of the employers shall not be permitted to interfere in the adjustments of the relations between the employers and employees.

18. Apprentices shall receive a salary of not less than 3 rubles [$1.55] per month during the first half year of their service, and not less than 6 rubles [$3.09] per month during the second half year of their service.

19. All conflicts between employers and employees shall be adjusted by means of special commissions.

20. Dismissals shall not be made without good cause.

21. All strikers shall be taken back into their old positions.

22. No dismissals shall be made until six months after the end of the strike.

23. The time of the strike shall be paid for.

ª The Jewish holiday begins in the evening, at the time of the setting of the sun and ends also at the setting of the sun; it is customary, therefore, for the small merchants to reopen their stores for the evening after the holiday.

24. Strike breakers shall be dismissed.

As a matter of course, political demands were also made, the significance of which was explained to the strikers. During the last few days before the beginning of the strikes special meetings were called at which the necessary advice was given as to how to present the demands, how to act during the strike, and so forth. On the 18th of June representatives of almost all the stores were called together and they were given circulars, containing the demands, for distribution among the strikers. At the hours appointed the stores began to close one after the other, and the salesmen and clerks gathered on the street. At the invitation of the non-Jewish workingmen, who are in sympathy with our organization, the stores of the Christians began to close up also.

That a general strike of the salesmen was in preparation could not long remain a secret—everybody in the town knew about it. Of course, the administration did not fail to take its usual measures. It increased its normal complement of police, called in troops, etc. * * * The assistant chief of the police personally visited the stores and asked the Christian salesmen not to join the "sheenies," for the "sheenies" organize strikes only out of love for riots, etc. Nevertheless, all stores closed that very day. The following day pickets were placed by us on all streets, whose duty it was to see that no salesmen returned to the stores. In several places it was found necessary to "take off" the strikers several times.

The city looked like a military camp. Patrols with loaded arms were to be found on all corners. Mounted police rode on the streets. The employers soon applied to the police for assistance. Arrests began. * * * These arrests could not but have considerable influence over the course of the strikes. A considerable portion of the salesmen who were less imbued with the consciousness of their interests was easily frightened. Other circumstances influenced the success of the strikes. On Sunday the Christian salesmen, whose affiliation with our organization was not very strong, returned to work. What was still worse, the employees of the ironware stores also returned to work. This became generally known, and many others began to contemplate returning to their offices. Nevertheless, the majority of stores remained closed on Sunday, and in most of those that were opened there were no salesmen except the employers themselves. Monday morning the employees of several stores of dress goods returned to work. The salesmen of other stores, especially of the dry-goods stores, kept up better, but it was generally felt that the strike was losing its spirit. The arrests continued. The strike lasted three or four days more, when negotiations began with many individual storekeepers. Monday morning one dry-goods store with over 60 employees satisfied almost all demands of the strikers; other stores made various concessions, some more, some less. In general it may be said that the strikers obtained the 12-hour day, while previous to that the salesmen worked at least $13\frac{1}{2}$ or 14 hours, and sometimes as many as 18 hours per day. They obtained 1 to $1\frac{1}{2}$ hours' recess for dinner, and in the larger stores the right of a 2-weeks' vacation with pay, and many other minor concessions.

In many respects the description of this strike is characteristic, if one remembers that it is written by an interested party. The many varied and, from a practical point of view, extravagant demands show that the object of the strike is not so much actual reform as the resulting political and economic agitation. It is, therefore, difficult to judge how far the strike was successful, for it is doubtful if the majority of the demands were made with a hope of their possible realization. It also shows how peculiar the position of the commercial employees is in a great many respects, in that it is necessary to fight against the performance of menial duties and against the interference of the wife of the employer in the treatment of the salesmen.

The history of most other strikes is similar to that just given. During the month of March, 1905, a strike of over 2,000 salesmen and other commercial employees was started by the Bund in Minsk. The demands formulated were as follows:

1. A 12-hour labor day (from 9 a. m. to 9 p. m.).
2. One-half hour interval for luncheon and one and one-half hour interval for dinner.
3. Closing of the stores on Saturday nights.
4. Weekly payment of wages.
5. Double wages four times a year, before the four chief Jewish holidays.
6. Polite treatment of all the employees.
7. The salesmen shall not be forced to perform menial duties.
8. The messengers shall not be obliged to carry heavy bundles.
9. Wages shall be paid for the entire time of the strike.
10. None of the strikers shall be discharged for participation in the strike.

The strike lasted ten days and ended with an almost complete victory for the strikers. All the demands were granted except demand 5; and in regard to demand 3, it was decided that during the four summer months the stores would not open on Saturday nights, while during the rest of the year the salesmen should be free on alternate Saturdays. This decision was reached at a combined meeting of the representatives of both parties to the struggle.

Similar strikes, more or less successful, have taken place in most of the larger cities of the Pale, with the result that at present a twelve-hour day, with one or two recesses, which bring the actual working day to ten hours, is the normal day of the commercial employee. These results have not been obtained in the many smaller towns and villages; but the number of commercial employees in these towns, in view of the petty nature of trade, is probably insignificant. The wages of the ordinary salesman or clerk are from an American point of view very small, 10 rubles ($5.15) a week being a fair compensation, while often as low as 5 or even 3 rubles ($2.58 or $1.55) a week are paid. It is probable, however, that the conditions of life of the majority of the commercial employees are better than are those of the mass of the petty traders described on a preceding page. These successful strikes have served to increase the strength and influence of the Bund among other social classes than the industrial workers.

PROFESSIONAL SERVICE.

The striving of the Russian Jew for a professional career has so well asserted itself during the comparatively short period of his life in the United States that it is surprising to find in Russia a very small percentage of the Jews in the professions, especially in view of the fact that all the universities in that country are state institutions, the tuition fee being small, and the great majority of the professional students coming from the poorer part of the city population. Altogether the number of Jews in the professions is 57,847 (not including the 14,103 persons who serve around churches, etc., given for comparative purposes in the tables of occupations), or a little more than 4 per cent of the Jews in gainful occupations. Even this number is to a great extent made up of an army of Hebrew teachers, consisting mostly of persons without any special training, who have failed in all other occupations and eke out a more miserable existence than even the average tailor or shoemaker. If the 35,273 persons constituting this army be disregarded, there is a remainder of only 22,574 in all the other professions—law, medicine, the ministry, government service, and service in public institutions.

The real cause of this seeming aversion of the Jew in Russia to a professional career, like so many features of Russian Jewish life, must be sought in the legal conditions of his existence. The relation of the Russian State to this problem, like its relation to the problem of Jewish agriculture, has undergone many changes. The practice of a profession usually requires a thorough special preparatory education. In the first half of the last century it was the avowed object of the Russian Government to attract the Jews into the higher schools of learning, that being rightly considered the best method to break up Jewish exclusiveness and help along the natural assimilation of the Jewish race. For many years this plan met with but moderate success, the older and more conservative Jews considering the Christian schools as institutions destructive of the Jewish religion and traditions, especially since the entering into those schools usually led of necessity to infringement upon the strict Jewish Sabbath and dietary laws. The pioneers of the younger generation, on going into the secular schools, had to meet the strenuous opposition of the other members of their families and often were forced to break family ties entirely.

Gradually, however, these prejudices gave way. But simultaneously with this change of feeling the attitude of the Government toward the problem of education of the Jews also changed. In the beginning of the eighties the proportion of Jews to be admitted to some schools was limited to a certain percentage of the students admitted. The growing number of Jewish students in the "gymnasiums" (high schools) and universities began to be looked upon with alarm. It was pointed out by opponents that the proportion of Jews was growing to be larger in the schools than in the population at large. The fact was disregarded that while constituting about 10 to 12 per cent of the population of the Pale, the Jews made up almost one-half of the population of the cities, which alone could be expected to furnish students of secondary and higher institutions of learning.

In the summer of 1887 the minister of instruction was empowered to limit the number of Jewish students to be admitted into the secondary institutions of learning. This limit was defined as 10 per cent for the institutions located within the Pale, 5 per cent in the remaining cities, and only 3 per cent in the two capital cities of Moscow and St. Petersburg: The measure was justified as necessary to maintain a more "normal proportion between the number of Jewish and Christian students." The result of this was that the classes in many classical and technical high schools remained half empty, for in the cities where the Jews constituted from 50 to 75 per cent of the population only 10 per cent of the high school boys could be of Jewish faith.

A full high school diploma is required to gain entrance to the university, yet it was found that many more Jewish than Christian boys were clamoring for admission. Besides, the effect of this limitation in regard to entrance into high schools could affect the university only in eight years, the course in the gymnasium lasting that long. The rule was therefore extended to the universities and other higher institutions of learning as well. The temporary rules have been enforced now for almost twenty years, but the number of Jewish applications for admission to the universities is still considerably larger than the number of vacancies provided for them, and hundreds of young men who can afford it, and a great many who really can not, throng the universities of Germany, Switzerland, France, Austria-Hungary, and even the United States and Italy. Only a small minority can avail itself of such an expedient.

The granting of so-called autonomy to Russian universities in September, 1905, raised the hope that the restrictions in regard to the admission of Jews to the schools, at least so far as the universities are concerned, would be abolished. As a matter of fact, in the fall of 1905 and 1906 some universities and technical schools disregarded all restrictions as established by the rules of 1887. The practice, however, was not universal. With the establishment of more normal conditions the question came up again. Recently the minister of public instruction has insisted upon the enforcement of the rules as they existed before autonomy was granted. In some institutions the old rules have therefore been applied in their entirety, in others the number of Jewish students admitted was above this legal limit. The ministry of public instruction permitted this accomplished infraction of the rules to stand, while insisting that such exceptions shall not be granted in the future. The situation therefore at present is about the same as it was before autonomy was granted.

More direct difficulties stand in the way of the Jews who try to enter the legal profession. While the admission of applicants to the bar according to the law depends upon local courts, since 1889 further admission to the bar of Jewish counselors at law is conditional upon a special permit of the minister of justice in each case.

As in the case of the limitation of the right of entering colleges, these restrictions were defended on the ground of the abnormal increase of the number of Jews in the professional schools of the universities. The practical Jew, it was said, did not care for higher education as such, but only for the lucrative profession to which a college education led. The extremely limited number of Jewish students in the purely scientific departments of the universities was claimed to prove this assertion. It should be said that very few can afford a purely scientific course in view of the fact that very few positions in the Government service are open to the Jews. The highly centralized system of Russian Government and the enormous administrative machine of Russia necessitate an army of Government employees, and Government service has always been the most popular profession of the educated classes in Russia. Besides, almost all the educational institutions are either governmental institutions or under Government supervision, and teaching in universities, colleges, and secondary, and even public schools is included under Government employment. Therefore not only an official but also a scientific or pedagogical career is out of the reach of the Jew in Russia.

Government employ has not been open to the Jews since 1828, but in the sixties some exceptions were made for Jews who received a medical education, the right of service in the medical department of the army having been given to them. Since 1882 the number of Jewish physicians and surgeons to be employed by the department has been limited to 5 per cent. While the law is not clear in regard to the teaching profession, there are no Jewish professors in the Russian universities, only a few docents, and no teachers in high schools and primary public schools for Christian pupils. Jewish teachers practice their profession only in special schools for Jews or in a few private institutions of learning.

It is customary in Russia to make a distinction between "Government service," i. e., service in the employ of the central Government, and "public service," i. e., service in local elective bodies or in the employ of the organs of local self-government, the "zemstvos," or the municipalities, etc. These latter institutions of self-government are also under the supervision of the central government, and the rights of the Jews in the domain of the public service are considerably curtailed. About the only important branch of public service in which Jews may receive appointments is the medical branch. The "zemstvos" (local self-government of the provinces and counties) employ a large number of physicians, druggists, nurses, and midwives to give gratuitous medical attendance to the peasants, and in this line of work persons of Jewish faith sometimes obtain appointments. These appointments are made by the zemstvos, but require the approval of the governors.

With so few opportunities in these avenues of employment, private practice of law and medicine remains almost the only field in which the educated Russian Jew may try his fortune. The result is an overcrowding of the professions, which is strongly felt in the towns of the Pale, where the general poverty of the masses reacts upon the earnings of the professional classes. Many graduate lawyers are forced to remain bank clerks at 10 rubles ($5.15) per week, and it is not unusual for physicians to receive only 30 to 40 kopecks (15 or 21 cents) for a visit at the patient's house. That the earnings of a practicing physician are not large is shown by the anxiety of the Jewish physicians to obtain the "zemstvo" positions spoken of above, which pay only 1,000 to 1,200 rubles ($515 to $618) a year. The graduates of the other schools usually make use of the right of living in the large cities outside of the Pale, and devote themselves to literature and journalism, the material returns being very moderate indeed. Cases of official change of religion are more frequent in Russia among professional persons and graduates of universities than among other classes of Jews, not only because the old bonds of religion are weakened but also because the material advantages to be obtained are greater.

PAUPERISM AND CHARITY.

PAUPERISM.

The insecurity of the earnings of the independent artisans, the low wages of the factory and small-shop employees, the petty business profits of the merchants and the extreme difficulty of finding employment after it is once lost, have all been indicated in the preceding pages, yet observers of the life in Jewish towns state that there are few professional paupers in comparison with the Russian towns, and that the paupers seen are usually either old and decrepit persons or children, that is, people who are unable to make a living.[a]

---

[a] See V Cherte Evreiskoy Osedlosti (In the Jewish Pale), by A. P. Subbotin. St. Petersburg, 1888, Vol. I, p. 134.

Even if the number of professional paupers, or persons who exist exclusively by private or public charity, is not so great among the Jews in Russia as one might expect, especially in view of the fact that professional pauperism is tolerated in that country, the number of the poor is extremely large, even interpreting the term "poor" in its narrower sense. In the broader sense of a person with an insufficient income, a person unable to make any savings and forced to live from hand to mouth, probably 90 per cent of the Russian Jews are poor. Robert Hunter says:

Poverty is a much broader term than pauperism. Those who are in poverty may be able to get a bare sustenance, but they are not able to obtain those necessaries which will permit them to maintain a state of physical efficiency.

Even this definition is perhaps somewhat too broad for our purpose. The poor as described therein are those persons who do not need to apply to charity, yet there are among the Jews in Russia a multitude of persons who occupy a middle ground. Not paupers "who depend upon public or private charity for sustenance" all the time, but persons who are not able to meet all the extraordinary expenses of the daily life, and who are therefore at intervals forced to apply, hateful as it may be to their feeling of self-respect, to public or private charity. Such extraordinary emergencies occur in the life of a poor Jewish family with distressing regularity, due to a peculiar cause, the religious holidays.

The Jewish holidays are not many, but they have an importance and holiness which, for the orthodox Jew, at least, make their fitting celebration an absolute law. These obligatory celebrations mean comparatively large expenditures of money, which a considerable number of the Jews are unable to meet, and it is then that the greatest amount of assistance is both given and received. It is noteworthy that so well is the exceptional nature of the occasion understood that the complaint has never been made that this form of charity leads to idleness and pauperism, or to destruction of self-respect. Some such principle guides one form of charity in the United States, namely, the Christmas dinners organized for the poor by various charitable organizations, notably the Salvation Army. But those dinners are admittedly for the benefit of the very poor, and consist in the direct administration of food in a fashion scarcely acceptable to the self-respecting poor, while in Russia a slight contribution of a few rubles to a family so as to enable it to celebrate in fitting fashion the holy days is considered more in the nature of a religious duty than a charitable act.

Even the ordinary "Shabees" (Sabbath) is a serious function with the orthodox. It demands not only absolute rest, but various observances in the way of special food, etc. The whole thought of the poor

Jew, and especially of the Jewish woman, during the week is directed to so manage as to be able to comply with the Sabbath requirements in a manner befitting a good Jew. That requires at least the regulation white bread, the fish, etc.; and the success of the week's work is judged by the ability to observe the Sabbath in the proper way. Then there is the Passover week, which is the only holiday to be compared in holiness to the Sabbath, and this period is a great deal more exacting than an ordinary Sabbath, so far as expenditure is concerned. It demands not only several days of interruption in work, but also many special dishes, the preparation of which is costly. Moreover, the demands of the Passover are absolutely peremptory. The religious law not only enjoins the eating of certain things during this week, but absolutely prohibits the eating of ordinary bread. There are other demands no less difficult of observance by the poorer Jews. In fact, the Jewish family that lives from hand to mouth often finds itself facing the approaching Passover absolutely unable to meet it according to the commands of the Hebraic law, and consequently in danger of committing a serious sin. Assistance of Jewish families during this season is the most common form of charitable work. At that time the Jewish people may truly be said to be divided into givers and receivers.

The data in regard to assistance distributed at that critical period are, therefore, the fullest possible measure of distress, the number immediately rising with every general fall in the prosperity of the people. The data were collected by the Jewish Colonization Society in its report, but the serious mistake was committed of broadly defining as paupers the entire number of people who applied for this kind of relief, of whom many often did not apply at all but customarily received some small sum.

Taken in this limited sense, as a measure of general distress but not of direct pauperism, the number of families receiving help for the Passover is nevertheless very significant. Information was obtained from more than 1,200 localities, containing over 700,000 families, and the families assisted reached the enormous number of 132,855, or almost 19 per cent. The proportion of families receiving assistance varied greatly as between different provinces, most of the Polish provinces showing a percentage as low as 14, while the three provinces of Lithuania give a percentage of 22. This agrees with the general observation, frequently emphasized in this article, that the Jews in Lithuania are probably lower in the economic scale than the Jews of any other part of the Pale, because the congestion of Jews is greatest there. Still more significant is the fact that the number of families assisted is rapidly growing. From many localities comparative data for several years have been obtained which conclusively show this rapid increase. By adding the data for all the localities for which information has been obtained it is found that within the short period of five years the number of families assisted had increased from 85,183 in 1894 to 108,922 families in 1898, an increase of 27.9 per cent. The amount of assistance given is usually small, sometimes falling as low as 75 copecks (39 cents), and, where the distribution of funds takes place through some organized agency, seldom exceeding 3 rubles ($1.55), a contribution which is not sufficient to put the recipients into the category of paupers.

Since this group of persons needing some assistance almost equals one-fifth of the total Jewish population of the Pale, all occupation groups have their representatives among them. An investigation in Odessa showed that the unskilled laborers were the most numerous recipients of this charity, but there was also a large number of artisans, such as tailors and shoemakers, as well as many persons who gained a precarious living from retail trade, peddlers, push-cart men and women.

CHARITABLE INSTITUTIONS.

The foregoing remarks refer to what might be called normal conditions, such as existed before the present anti-Jewish sentiment manifested itself.

The assistance by means of a small payment before the Passover being the most frequent form of charitable work serves best as a measure of the extent of the need for charity, but it by no means represents all of the charitable work needed or given in the Pale. On the contrary, the charitable institutions are numerous and varied.

It is well known that when two hundred and fifty years ago the first Jews applied for permission to come into North America, namely, into New Amsterdam, they were granted the permission under the condition that they care for their own poor—a condition they have faithfully kept. It was scarcely necessary to exact that condition, for the care of the poor is a characteristic feature of the Jewish people. Though the Russian Jews were an integral part of the population of the region in which they lived long before the time they came under the domination of the Russian Government, the Russian code of laws contains a similar provision in regard to the Jews and their poor.

This demand could have been made only because of the special Jewish communal organizations which exist in the towns of the Pale, and which are not only recognized by law but intrusted with certain powers and duties, the most important of which, from an economic point of view, being the collection of taxes. A series of special taxes, direct as well as indirect, have been established (the principal one being the tax on meat) for the purpose of supplying the community with means to do charitable work, support schools, hospitals, etc. The amount and the objects of the tax, in addition to the indirect tax on meat, are determined by the community under the supervision and with the approval of the authorities, but the tax is not collected directly by the community; it is rented out at auction, also with the approval of the administration. The tax, therefore, must bring an income, not only to the community but also to the lessor. Moreover, the actual distribution of the sums collected is not intrusted to the Jewish community, but to the local authorities. The budget must be approved by the governor of the province. Unnecessary economy in the distribution of the funds usually results and large sums are transferred to the public treasury, after which an application for these funds to be used for charitable enterprises must have the approval of the ministry of finance.

The income from these special taxes, nevertheless, remains a very important item of the budgets of the various charitable institutions, but no less important are the private contributions and those of the various nonofficial charitable organizations.

The following statement shows the number of each of the most common types of charitable organization known among the Jews in Russia:

Societies for general relief	290
Hospitals and dispensaries	112
Committees for the care of the sick	665
Homes for the old and the infirm	126
Lodging houses and houses of refuge for strangers	180
Societies for noninterest-bearing loans	350
Societies for distribution of food	500
Societies for distribution of clothing	72
Societies for assisting poor brides	51
Total	2,346

The variety and number of relief societies is characteristic not only of the great need for them but also of the charitable traditions of the Jews.

The divers functions of these charitable organizations are of special interest to the American, because many similar organizations, though usually on a much larger scale than in Russia, have been established in the United States by the Jewish immigrants, who thus introduce types of relief little known to the American charity worker. It is well, therefore, to begin with the description of these specialized institutions.

Perhaps the most important from an economic point of view are the institutions for gratuitous credit. The high cost of credit in the Pale is a serious cause of distress, since the smallest loan may often lead a self-supporting family to financial ruin. It may not be difficult for the petty trader or the artisan to obtain a small loan, but the conditions are usually onerous. The money lender charges exorbitant interest, which may reach 20, 30, or even 60 per cent. The following is a typical case:

An artisan borrows 50 rubles ($25.75), with an agreement to pay up in weekly installments of 1 ruble (51.5 cents) per week; but the interest, amounting to 12 rubles ($6.18), is deducted from the loan at the time it is made, only 38 rubles ($19.57) being actually received by the borrower, and under the plan of paying the loan in weekly installments, covering principal and interest, the rate of interest amounts to about 59 per cent per annum.

In 1895, by a special law, the formation of small societies for mutual credit was facilitated, and by 1902 there were within the Pale 50 societies of that nature, in which the Jews constituted the predominating element. But since that year the authorities have demanded that two-thirds of the board of directors of all such new societies shall consist of Christian men and that the chairman shall be a Christian. These limitations have effectively stopped the increase in the number of Jewish credit societies of the mutual kind, and have emphasized the necessity for the charitable institutions.

It is characteristic that of the 350 loan societies 205, or 58.6 per cent, are found in northwestern Russia, not only because the need for them is greater there, but because the communal feeling and social activity is much greater in that region.

The revenues, and therefore the range of activity, of these societies are very small. Of 253 organizations for which the amount of capital was given 77 had less than 100 rubles ($51.50) each, 112 had from 100 to 500 rubles ($51.50 to $257.50) each, 38 had from 500 to 1,000 rubles ($257.50 to $515) each, and only 26 had over 1,000 rubles ($515) each. The resources being so limited, the loans range from 3 to 15 rubles ($1.55 to $7.73), and seldom exceed 25 rubles ($12.88). Yet, in its conception, it is a useful method of granting relief. Several large organizations of this kind exist in New York City. Some of these societies require security in the shape of valuables, others require the guaranty of some well-to-do person, but the rule is not to charge any interest for the loan. The most significant feature of these organizations is that they are not established by the private munificence of some one person, but by means of small contributions from almost all the members of the local Jewish community, the contributions sometimes being not greater than 25 kopecks (13 cents) per annum.

There is nothing especially interesting to be said in regard to the 112 Jewish hospitals existing in the Jewish cities of the Pale. Besides the general insufficiency of hospital facilities in Russian towns, there is the important consideration of the religious dietary laws, which make separate Jewish hospitals necessary. There are a few hospitals endowed by private charity, but most of these institutions are supported out of the special taxes spoken of above. Most of the large hospitals are located in the South and Southwest, and while northwestern Russia has a greater share of all other charitable institutions, it has only a few hospitals. A hospital is an establishment that annually requires a large sum of money for its support, and few northwestern towns can afford to make the necessary outlay.

The lack of hospitals in the Northwest is partly compensated by numerous societies for the care of the sick at their homes. Out of a total of 665 such societies 349 are located in the northwestern, 143 in the southern and the southwestern, and 173 in the Polish provinces. The functions of these circles are varied, ranging from financial assistance and hiring of medical help to actual care of the sick by members of the circle. The budget of such a circle seldom exceeds 500 rubles ($257.50) each year.

The organizations for furnishing food to the needy at a nominal compensation, or absolutely free, are not many and exist mainly in the larger cities. Thus, the dining room for the poor in Vilna distributes during the year about 200,000 dinners, at the average cost to itself of 8 or 9 kopecks (4.1 or 4.6 cents), while the price charged is 3 or 5 kopecks (1.5 or 2.6 cents). This is the result of an effort to substitute organized assistance for the traditional custom of having some poor person at one's table, a custom that is still observed in the smaller towns, and is a form of charity specially popular during the most important holidays, when one or two poor persons are to be seen at the tables of the richest men of the town each Saturday, if not every day. The poor scholars of the "kheders" and of the "eshiboths" (institutions for higher instruction in the Hebrew language and Jewish theology) are the most frequent recipients of this primitive form of charity, but the practice is rapidly dying out. It was customary for such poor students to make their way through the school by boarding at seven places, one day a week at each place. Another form of charity, which is rapidly vanishing, is the assistance to poor brides. This consists in small subsidies, sometimes limited to 5 rubles ($2.58) for the purchase of the most necessary household utensils. Since marriage is strongly urged on each and every Jewish youth and maiden, it is considered a holy act to assist poor girls to its consummation.

The more primitive charitable institutions are centered around the local synagogue, because charitable activity has among all nations found its inception in the religious feeling, but the more modern organizations are managed by special boards and committees, and are frequently incorporated. But no matter how the organization is effected, practically each Jewish family, unless it be itself a recipient of charity, contributes to some charitable purpose, even if it be

16251—08——12

only 2 copecks (1 cent) a week, this sum not infrequently being the regular dues in some of the societies of the smaller towns. Even a superficial acquaintance with the life of the Russian Jews in the large American cities shows the same tendencies to mutual help and self-help to a marked degree, the desire to take care of its own poor and sick being still strong in the Jewish race.

EDUCATIONAL OPPORTUNITIES.

The economic importance of popular education is so well recognized that no apology is necessary for introducing the subject of education in a study of economic conditions.

The degree of literacy may be considered a fair measure of the educational standing of a people. It is therefore proper to begin the study of education of the Russian Jews by quoting the available data of the degree of literacy among them.

According to the Russian census of 1897 there were in a population of 125,640,021 persons, 26,569,585 literate persons, or 21.1 per cent. The number of males who could read and write was 18,318,812 out of a total of 62,477,348, or 29.3 per cent, while the number of literate females was 8,250,773 out of 63,162,673, or 13.1 per cent. Thus the degree of Russian illiteracy is not so great as frequent assertions in the press would make it appear, for one often sees the statement that more than 90 per cent of the Russian people can neither read nor write. Moreover, the proportion stated above does not take into consideration the large number of children of tender age, who should certainly be excluded in calculating the percentage of illiteracy.

But the point which must be emphasized here is that the proportion of illiterate persons of Jewish faith is much smaller. Of 5,215,805 persons of Jewish faith there were 2,031,497 literate persons, or 39 per cent, which gives a per cent of literacy almost double that of the total population of Russia. Of 2,547,144 males, 1,259,248, or 49.4 per cent, were literate, while of 2,668,661 females, 772,249, or only 29 per cent, could read. Thus the proportionate literacy of the Jews is about twice as high as that of the entire Russian nation.

A better idea of the degree of literacy and illiteracy among the Jews, in comparison to the entire population of the Russian Empire, may be obtained by means of a table giving the number and per cent of persons able to read, by age groups. These data are presented in the table following. Unfortunately the basis for this table in the reports of the Russian census is not religion, but nationality as determined by the mother tongue. As a result about two hundred thousand Jews of the higher, more educated classes, who claimed

Russian as their mother tongue, have been excluded, which un-doubtedly reduces the actual percentage of Jewish persons able to read.

LITERACY OF THE TOTAL RUSSIAN POPULATION AND OF THE JEWISH POPULA-
TION IN EACH SPECIFIED AGE GROUP, BY SEX, 1897.

[From Premier Recensement Général de la Population de l'Empire de Russie, 1897.]

Age group.	All Russia.			Jews.		
	Total population.	Literates.		Total.	Literates.	
		Number.	Per cent of total population.		Number.	Per cent of total Jews.
MALES.						
Under 1 year....................	2,155,199	....	......	82,607	....	......
1 to 9 years....................	14,975,808	789,489	5.3	637,496	77,781	12.2
10 to 19 years..................	13,094,402	5,955,693	45.5	563,622	336,863	59.8
20 to 29 years..................	10,145,066	4,552,412	44.9	414,791	294,365	71.0
30 to 39 years..................	7,893,941	3,118,509	39.5	284,037	198,413	69.9
40 to 49 years..................	5,873,596	1,950,533	33.2	196,560	132,620	67.5
50 to 59 years..................	4,110,800	1,087,720	26.5	148,672	91,555	61.6
60 years or over................	4,202,616	858,322	20.2	142,684	77,452	54.3
Age unknown....................	25,920	6,134	23.7	926	442	47.7
Total.....................	62,477,348	18,318,812	29.3	2,471,395	1,209,491	48.9
10 years of age or over..........	45,346,341	17,529,323	38.7	1,751,292	1,131,710	64.6
FEMALES.						
Under 1 year....................	2,136,542	....	......	79,270	....	......
1 to 9 years....................	15,071,969	461,097	3.1	639,006	44,222	6.9
10 to 19 years..................	13,359,380	2,915,494	21.8	646,552	282,590	43.7
20 to 29 years..................	10,215,904	1,995,914	19.5	429,693	195,953	45.6
30 to 39 years..................	7,912,107	1,245,535	15.7	294,282	100,458	34.1
40 to 49 years..................	5,832,868	735,910	12.6	214,246	55,013	25.7
50 to 59 years..................	4,210,657	465,619	11.1	159,283	32,029	20.1
60 years or over................	4,398,724	428,056	9.7	128,588	19,182	14.9
Age unknown....................	24,522	3,158	12.9	841	219	26.0
Total.....................	63,162,673	8,250,773	13.1	2,591,761	729,666	28.2
10 years of age or over..........	45,954,162	7,789,676	17.0	1,873,485	685,444	36.6
BOTH SEXES.						
Under 1 year....................	4,291,741	....	......	161,877	....	......
1 to 9 years....................	30,047,777	1,250,586	4.1	1,276,502	122,003	9.6
10 to 19 years..................	26,453,782	8,871,187	33.5	1,210,174	619,453	51.2
20 to 29 years..................	20,360,970	6,548,326	32.2	844,484	490,318	58.1
30 to 39 years..................	15,806,048	4,364,044	27.6	578,319	298,871	51.7
40 to 49 years..................	11,706,464	2,686,443	22.9	410,806	187,633	45.7
50 to 59 years..................	8,321,457	1,553,339	18.7	307,955	123,584	40.1
60 years or over................	8,601,340	1,286,378	15.0	271,272	96,634	35.6
Age unknown....................	50,442	9,292	18.4	1,767	661	37.4
Total.....................	125,640,021	26,569,585	21.1	5,063,156	1,939,157	38.3
10 years of age or over..........	91,300,503	25,318,999	27.7	3,624,777	1,817,154	50.1

The following deductions may be made from the above table: Of those over 10 years of age the illiteracy among the Jews is con-siderably smaller than for the total population of the Russian Empire, it being 72.3 per cent for the entire country, and only 49.9 per cent for the Jews. For the male population over 10 years of age the com-parative figures of illiteracy are: For the total 61.3 per cent, and for the Jews only 35.4 per cent. For the female population over 10 years of age the data of illiteracy are: For the total 83 per cent, and for the Jews 63.4 per cent.

When, however, the table is examined carefully it is found, both for the total population and for the Jews, that the lower the age of the class the higher is the percentage of literacy. This indicates an improving condition in Russia. The rise is more noticeable in the case of the total population, which seems to indicate that within recent years the cause of education has received greater stimulus among the Russian population than among the Jews.

Some slight rise is noticed also among the Jews, especially among women, the education of the latter being comparatively an innovation. Nevertheless, it is worthy of notice that the highest age group among the Jews has a larger percentage of people able to read than the most educated total age group, there being proportionately more literate Jews over 60 years old than literate Russian population of the age of 10 to 19 years. In other words, fifty years ago the educational standard of the Jews was higher than that of the Russian people at large is at present. This comparison is certainly very significant.

It must be added that the data are ten years old, and that the general rise of education must have further reduced the percentage of illiterates among the Jews and among other persons in Russia.

This comparatively high standard of education, achieved, as will be shown presently, without any system of State obligatory schools, is to a great extent due to the religious spirit of the Jews. The ability to read his prayers is as sacred to the Jew of the older generation as it was to the New Englander of the colonial times and had the same effect of stimulating education. It follows that the majority of the Jews first learn to read the Hebrew alphabet; and since the same alphabet is used for the so-called Yiddish (a German dialect, the colloquial language of the Jewish mass), therefore the Jew who can read his prayers has the ability to read and write in his spoken tongue.

The vast majority of the Jews, and especially the Jews in the cities of the Pale, where they constitute the majority of the population, speak this Yiddish, but the mingling with persons who speak other tongues forces upon the average Jew a knowledge of some other language. The enforced use of Russian in all Government institutions makes some knowledge of Russian almost a necessity, and so, nolens volens, a great number of the Jews derive what additional culture there is to be obtained from a knowledge of a second language. In the following table are presented the data in regard to the number and per cent of Jews of all the age groups who can read Russian.

NUMBER AND PER CENT OF JEWS IN EACH SPECIFIED AGE GROUP ABLE TO READ RUSSIAN, BY SEX, 1897.

[From Premier Recensement Général de la Population de l'Empire de Russie, 1897.]

Age group.	Males.			Females.			Both sexes.		
	Total.	Able to read Russian.		Total.	Able to read Russian.		Total.	Able to read Russian.	
		Number.	Per cent.		Number.	Per cent.		Number.	Per cent.
1 to 9 years	637,496	40,385	6.3	639,006	31,520	4.9	1,276,502	71,905	5.6
10 to 19 years	563,622	237,947	42.2	646,552	204,648	31.7	1,210,174	442,595	36.6
20 to 29 years	414,791	217,984	52.5	429,693	127,737	29.7	844,484	345,721	40.9
30 to 39 years	284,037	137,615	48.4	294,282	52,484	17.8	578,319	190,099	32.9
40 to 49 years	196,560	79,674	40.5	214,246	20,931	9.8	410,806	100,605	24.5
50 to 59 years	148,672	46,302	31.1	159,283	9,677	6.1	307,955	55,979	18.2
60 years or over	142,684	31,777	22.3	128,588	4,657	3.6	271,272	36,434	13.4
Age unknown	926	315	34.0	841	133	15.8	1,767	448	25.4
Total	2,388,788	791,999	33.2	2,512,491	451,787	17.9	4,901,279	1,243,786	25.4
10 years of age or over.	1,751,292	751,614	42.9	1,873,485	420,267	22.5	3,624,777	1,171,881	32.1

Thus it is found that more than two-fifths of the males 10 years of age or over, and almost one-fourth of the females of the same age group, are able to read Russian. This feature of education is comparatively new, since the figures show that the percentage is larger among the lower than among the higher age periods. The age period of from 20 to 29 is the most characteristic among the males, 52.5 per cent being able to read Russian, while among the females 10 to 19 is the age period that shows the greatest proportion, 31.7 per cent being able to read that language.

To appreciate these results achieved by the Jews of the Pale within a very short time it is necessary to know something of the educational system as it exists in Russia. A system of gratuitous education supplied to all by the Government is an institution comparatively new to Russia. High schools and universities were established by the Government long before there were any schools for the common people. The emancipation of the serfs in 1861 found the Russians an illiterate people. It was only after the Government had established the so-called "zemstvos" that an organized effort was made to introduce schools in the rural districts, and the granting of some measure of municipal self-government to the cities gave the first impetus to the city schools. No such institutions were granted to the western Provinces of the Pale, because the foreign population was not trusted with such rights; therefore the Jew in Russia has never enjoyed the benefits of a general gratuitous governmental system of education.

While this may be considered a passive infringement of the Jew's opportunity for an elementary education, there have existed and still exist many other restrictions of a more direct kind. The limitations, by percentages, of Jewish students admitted to universities and high schools have been pointed out in the section on professional service. These restrictions exist even for private high schools, which are subject to governmental supervision in the same degree as governmental institutions.

To provide for the education of the Jewish children, who are thus almost debarred from the general schools, a few special Government schools are established, but these schools depend upon a limited fund and the number is very insufficient. The number of such schools at the end of the last century was determined to be 183, with an average of 113 pupils for each school. Two teachers' institutes for the preparation of Jewish teachers were established, but one of them was subsequently discontinued.

Without the benefits of a system of free education the Jews are forced to depend upon their own resources. Private schools and communal schools established and supported by charitable or other organizations have been opened in many places, the number of such schools with systematic courses being 637, so that the total number of schools in Russia for the Jews is 820.

But the number of schools in itself does not give a proper conception of the lack of educational facilities; much depends upon the size of the schools. The total number of pupils in these schools was determined to be about 50,000, and if the inevitable omissions are considered the number may be as great as 60,000; but if the number of children of school age be estimated at one-seventh of the total population (which is a very small proportion), it follows that out of more than 700,000 children less than 10 per cent enjoy the privilege of schooling in more or less organized schools, which, on the whole, have a course of studies lower in grade than that of a grammar school in the United States.

The Russian Jews owe their comparatively low degree of illiteracy to the peculiar Jewish institution called the "kheder," a denominational school the primary object of which is instruction in the Bible and in Jewish religion and learning. In practice this takes the form of instruction in the Hebrew language and in reading the Scriptures and the many commentaries. If the specific name of these schools has come to be used in the Russian language, it is because of the many peculiarities of their organization, which peculiarities have been preserved from time immemorial.

The "kheder" is a private school. The State interests itself little in the organization of these "kheders" beyond requiring that no person shall teach in them without a permit, and that he shall not teach anything but Jewish subjects. Practically no requirements of an educational nature are enforced. The profession of a "melamed," as a teacher in one of these "kheders" is called, has therefore become the refuge of men who have failed in other occupations. A "melamed" organizes the school, and upon his energy and facilities depends the number of scholars that can be gathered into it.

An investigation conducted by the well-known Imperial Russian Free Economic Society in 1894 determined the number of "kheders" at 14,740, with 202,000 pupils, or an average of 13.7 pupils per "kheder." This gives an idea of the nature of the school. The Jewish Colonization Society collated data from 507 localities, with a Jewish population of 1,420,000, and found 7,145 "kheders," from which data it estimates the total number of existing "kheders" to be 24,000. Taking the average number of pupils to each "kheder" to be 13.7, these 24,000 "kheders" evidently contained about 329,000 pupils.

The investigation of the Russian Free Economic Society showed that in 1894, out of a total of 201,964 pupils registered in the 14,740 "kheders" reported, there were only 10,459 girls, or 5.2 per cent. It seems, then, that almost all the boys of school age attend a "kheder," while only a few girls do so. It is true that the religious element plays some part in this unequal distribution of the educational advantages, the church duties of the Jewish men being more important than those of the women. For the same reason the old-fashioned Jew of the Pale is readier to send his daughter than his son to a secular, Christian school. As has been shown above, the facilities for giving the Jewish child an education in the governmental schools are extremely limited, and while the percentage of illiteracy among the Jewish women is much higher than among the men, still the data in regard to the number of girls attending schools do not show where the 45 per cent of young Jewish women acquired an elementary education, and, what is still more surprising, where 35 to 40 per cent of them acquired a knowledge of Russian in addition to Yiddish.

The explanation lies probably in the peculiar zeal of the Jewish people for some education, for there is scarcely another race or social group which has succeeded in attaining such a high percentage of literacy without a public school system. The women and girls use every available means to learn to read and write. Private tutoring is very popular in Russia, and because of the general low standard of prosperity such tutoring has been made so inexpensive as to be within the means of even poor families, the average Jewish family being willing to sacrifice a great deal to obtain some education. Then, again, the male members of the family will share their education the best way they know how with their sisters. The very widespread tendency of the educated minority to organize secret classes for the instruction of adult working men and women in combination with secret socialist and other propaganda must not be disregarded, although no statistical accounting of the dimensions of this movement is possible. Yet there is evidence in the tables of the existence of this belated education. It will be noticed that for the total population of Russia the age period of from 10 to 19 is the one that shows the highest percentage of people able to read, while among the Jews it is, on the contrary, the age period of from 20 to 29, and the difference between this age period and the one immediately preceding is 2 per cent among the females and as much as 11 per cent among the males. If the natural progress of educational facilities be taken into additional consideration, it follows that the percentage of persons acquiring the ability to read and write many years after the passing of the school period is even greater than the percentages given above indicate. The same tendency is noticed in the overcrowded night schools of New York City.

Still the "kheder" remains the most important educational institution of the Jewish Pale. In the absence of other and better facilities the "kheder" has an important function to fulfill. It does not follow that it does it in a satisfactory manner, the "melamed" having in the majority of cases neither the fitness nor the facilities for successful teaching. The methods are antiquated and the environments indescribably bad. The facilities of the schoolroom may be imagined, or at least guessed at, if one remembers that the tuition fees from 15 to 20 pupils are the only source of income of the "melamed;" and in view of the poverty of his clients these tuition fees can not amount to much. Yet, while the income of the "melamed" is small, the expense of education is a heavy burden to a poor family with several children of school age. For a half-year term the average tuition fees vary from 10 to 15 rubles ($5.15 to $7.73) for the younger pupils, and from 12 to 25 rubles ($6.18 to $12.88) for the older and more advanced pupils. The fees are usually higher in the large cities and lower in the small settlements, the average being about 25 rubles ($12.88) a year in the former and 18 rubles ($9.27) a year in the latter. Such fees scarcely provide the "melamed" with an income of 200 to 300 rubles ($103 to $154.50) a year, therefore the hiring of special premises for school purposes is out of the question, and the dwelling of the "melamed" is at the same time the school. Only in about 20 per cent of the schools investigated was a separate room specially provided in the house of the teacher. In the remaining 80 per cent the schoolroom was the living room of the teacher's family, which was at the same time the sleeping room, the kitchen, etc. The furnishings of a typical "kheder" are limited to a long table provided on both sides with plain wooden benches, so high that the children's feet hang down without touching the floor, because the teacher can not afford to provide the children of different ages with benches of different heights. Usually there is not even a back to lean on, and the children are forced to bend over the table through the long school day. The air in this improvised schoolroom has often been described as killing. During the winter months the dearth of fuel necessitates keeping the windows closed, and the air is vitiated not only by the overcrowding of the room with pupils but also by the cooking of food. All these objectionable features of the typical "kheder" are accentuated by the excessively long hours, almost as excessive as were the hours in the factory before the struggle of the Bund for a shorter workday began. The antiquated methods of instruction, together with the zeal of the parents that their son understand the intricacies of Bible exegetics at the time when the American boy has scarcely advanced beyond the second reader, encourage these long hours. The school day begins at 9 a. m. and ends at 5, sometimes at 6 or even at 8 p. m., so that the school day lasts anywhere from eight to eleven hours. Only in the larger cities, especially of the South, where the Jewish traditions are weakened and Jewish learning not held in such esteem, does the school day sometimes fall to seven hours. When the Jewish boy spends the entire day for many years, and practically without any vacation, in this atmosphere in the strenuous mental effort of disentangling the medieval intricacies of the commentators of the Bible, there is little wonder that he leaves the "kheder" an anæmic, emaciated youth, with physical powers much impaired.

The "talmud-thora" is a communal school, supported by the Jewish community, in which an effort is made to do away with the hygienic and educational imperfections of the "kheder" system. The Hebrew branches are given sufficient prominence to make the school satisfactory to the orthodox, while at the same time are introduced the Russian language and some general educational subjects. The "talmud-thora" is gradually growing into a national school for the Jews; but the number of these institutions is limited, because of their general expensiveness.

An improvement of the school facilities for the Jews in Russia will come only after the many restrictions are abolished and with substantial assistance from the Government funds.

The facts detailed in the foregoing pages indicate how deeply the lives of the Russian Jews have been influenced by the legal conditions under which they live. A study of these conditions and their economic results seems to be doubly important for a clear understanding of Russian Jewish immigration to this country; not only because these conditions shape the physical, psychological, and economic status of the immigrant, but also because they are of decisive influence in determining the very dimensions of the current of immigration from Western Russia to the United States.

The Modern
Jewish Experience

An Arno Press Collection

Asch, Sholem. **Kiddush Ha-Shem**: An Epic of 1648. 1926

Benjamin, I⌈srael ben⌉ J⌈oseph⌉. **Three Years in America:**
1859-1862. 1956. Two vols. in one.

Berman, Hannah. **Melutovna.** 1913

Besant, Walter. **The Rebel Queen.** 1893

Blaustein, David. **Memoirs of David Blaustein.** 1913

Brandes, George. **Reminiscences of My Childhood and Youth.** 1906

Brinig, Myron. **Singermann.** 1929

Cahan, A⌈braham⌉. **The White Terror and the Red.** 1905

Chotzinoff, Samuel. **A Lost Paradise.** 1955

Cohen, Morris Raphael. **A Dreamer's Journey.** 1949

Cowen, Philip. **Memories of an American Jew.** 1932

Cooper, Samuel W. **Think and Thank.** 1890

Davitt, Michael. **Within the Pale.** 1903

Dembitz, Lewis N. **Jewish Services in Synagogue and Home.** 1898

Epstein, Jacob. **Epstein:** An Autobiography. 1955

Ferber, Edna. **Fanny Herself.** 1917

Fineman, Irving. **Hear, Ye Sons.** 1933

Fishberg, Maurice. **The Jews:** A Study of Race and Environment. 1911

Fleg, Edmond. **Why I Am a Jew.** 1945

Franzos, Karl Emil. **The Jews of Barnow.** 1883

Gamoran, Emanuel. **Changing Conceptions in Jewish Education.** 1924

Glass, Montagu. **Potash and Perlmutter.** 1909

Goldmark, Josephine. **Pilgrims of '48.** 1930

Grossman, Leonid Petrovich. **Confession of a Jew.** 1924

Gratz, Rebecca. **Letters of Rebecca Gratz.** 1929

Kelly, Myra. **Little Aliens.** 1910

Klein, A. M. **Poems.** 1944

Kober, Arthur. **Having Wonderful Time.** 1937

Kohut, Rebekah. **My Portion** (An Autobiography). 1925

Leroy-Beaulieu, Anatole. **Israel Among the Nations.** 1904

Levin, Shmarya. **Childhood in Exile.** 1929

Levin, Shmarya. **Youth in Revolt.** 1930

Levin, Shmarya. **The Arena.** 1932

Levy, Esther. **Jewish Cookery Book on Principles of Economy Adapted for Jewish Housekeepers.** 1871

Levy, Harriet Lane. **920 O'Farrell Street.** 1947

Lewisohn, Ludwig. **Mid-Channel.** 1929

Lewisohn, Ludwig. **The Island Within.** 1928

Markens, Isaac. **The Hebrews in America.** 1888

Martens, Frederick H. **Leo Ornstein.** 1918

Meade, Robert Douthat. **Judah P. Benjamin.** 1943

Mendoza, Daniel. **The Memoirs of the Life of Daniel Mendoza.** 1951

Meredith, George. **The Tragic Comedians.** 1922

Nichols, Anne. **Abie's Irish Rose.** 1927

Nordau, Max. **The Conventional Lies of Our Civilization.** 1895

Nyburg, Sidney L. **The Chosen People.** 1917

Pinski, David. **Three Plays.** 1918

Roth, Cecil. **A History of the Marranos.** 1932

Roth, Cecil. **A Life of Menasseh Ben Israel.** 1934

Rubinow, I[saac] M. **Economic Conditions of the Jews in Russia.** 1907

Sabsovich, Katherine. **Adventures in Idealism.** 1922

Sachs, A[braham] S. **Worlds That Passed.** 1928

Seide, Michael. **The Common Thread.** 1944

Steiner, Edward A. **From Alien to Citizen.** 1914

Untermeyer, Louis. **Roast Leviathan.** 1923

Weinstein, Gregory. **The Ardent Eighties.** 1928

Yezierska, Anzia. **Hungry Hearts.** 1920

Yiddish Tales. 1912

Zangwill, Israel. **The Melting-Pot.** 1932

Zunser, Eliakum. **Selected Songs of Eliakum Zunser.** 1928